THE l

MW01284933

NORWEGIAN PHRASE BOOK

1001 NORWEGIAN PHRASES FOR BEGINNERS AND BEYOND!

BY ADRIAN GEE

ISBN: 979-8-871227-65-7

Author's Note

Welcome to "The Ultimate Norwegian Phrase Book"! I am overjoyed to be your guide on this enchanting journey through the Norwegian language, a tongue celebrated for its lyrical beauty and the rich tapestry of its cultural heritage. Whether you are mesmerized by the majestic fjords, inspired by the tranquil beauty of Norway's landscapes, or fascinated by the nation's storied history and vibrant traditions, this book is meticulously designed to make your linguistic journey as enriching and enjoyable as possible.

As a dedicated linguist and a proponent of deep cultural engagement, I understand the intricate nuances involved in mastering a new language. This book is born from that understanding, intended to be your reliable guide as you sail towards Norwegian fluency.

Connect with Me: Learning a language goes beyond mere memorization of vocabulary and grammar—it's an exciting voyage into connecting with people and immersing in the essence of a unique culture. I warmly invite you to join me and fellow language enthusiasts on Instagram: @adriangruszka. This platform serves as a lively space for exchanging knowledge and experiences.

Sharing is Caring: If this book plays a key role in your language learning journey, I would be immensely grateful for your recommendation to others who cherish the linguistic diversity of our world. I encourage you to share your progress and milestones in Norwegian on Instagram and tag me! I look forward to celebrating each step of your progress with you!

Embarking on the path to learning Norwegian is akin to stepping into a world of natural wonder, rich history, and a welcoming community spirit. Embrace the challenges, revel in your advancements, and savor every moment of your Norwegian adventure.

Lykke til! (Good luck!)

-Adrian Gee

CONTENTS

INTRODUCTION

Velkommen! (Welcome!)

Whether you're envisioning the awe-inspiring vistas of Norway's fjords, preparing to wander the historic streets of Bergen, eager to connect with Norwegian speakers, or simply learning Norwegian out of a love for its melodic charm, this phrase book is crafted to be your faithful companion.

Embarking on the journey of learning Norwegian opens the door to a world marked by its breathtaking natural beauty, profound historical depth, and the warm, welcoming ethos of Norwegian life.

Hvorfor Norsk? (Why Norwegian?)

With approximately 5 million native speakers, Norwegian is not just the language of the spectacular Aurora Borealis and the legendary Vikings, but it also plays a vital role in Scandinavian culture, commerce, and innovation. As the official language of Norway, it is an indispensable tool for travelers, business professionals, and all who are drawn to its distinctive charm.

Uttale (Pronunciation)

Before diving into the rich variety of phrases and expressions, it's crucial to acquaint yourself with the rhythmic beauty of Norwegian. Each language has its own unique melody, and Norwegian flows with a cadence that is both soft and vibrant, echoing the essence of its landscapes and seascapes. Initially, the pronunciation might appear challenging, but with practice, the clear tones and characteristic inflections of Norwegian can enrich your language learning experience.

Norwegian pronunciation is known for its clarity and tonal variations. The distinct enunciation of words, the light roll of 'r's, and the melodic intonation set it apart from other languages. Mastering pronunciation not only aids in clear communication but also deepens your bond with the people and the rich traditions of Norway.

Norsk Alfabet (The Norwegian Alphabet)

The Norwegian alphabet, rooted in the Latin script, comprises 29 letters. Like Swedish, it includes some pronunciations that might be unfamiliar to English speakers, and features three additional letters unique to Norwegian and certain other Nordic languages.

Vokaler (Vowels)

A (a): Similar to the "a" in "father."
E (e): Can be like the "e" in "bed," or akin to the "ai" in "fair."
I (i): Resembles the "ee" in "see."
O (o): Varies between the "o" in "more" and the "oo" in "book."
U (u): Comparable to the "oo" in "food."
Y (y): Like the French "u" in "lune" or German "ü" in "füssen," with rounded lips.
Æ (æ): Sounds like the "a" in "cat."
Ø (ø): Similar to the "i" in "bird" or the "eu" in French "peur."
Å (å): Resembles the "o" in "more" or the "au" in "Paul."

Konsonanter (Consonants)

B (b): As in English "bat."
C (c): Primarily found in loanwords, often pronounced like "s" or "k" depending on the origin of the word.
D (d): Similar to the "d" in "dog."
F (f): As in English "far."

G (g): Generally like the "g" in "go," but before "i" or "y," it sounds like "y" in "yes."
H (h): Like the English "h" in "hat."
J (j): Similar to the "y" in "yes."
K (k): Like the "k" in "kite."
L (l): As in English "love."
M (m): Like the English "m" in "mother."
N (n): Like the "n" in "nice."
P (p): As in English "pen."
Q (q): Rare in Norwegian, typically found in loanwords, pronounced as "kw."
R (r): A rolling "r," pronounced at the front of the mouth.
S (s): Like the "s" in "see."
T (t): Like the "t" in "top."
V (v): Like the "v" in "victory."
W (w): Rare in Norwegian and often found in loanwords, pronounced like "v" or "w" in English depending on origin.
X (x): Usually pronounced as "ks," as in "box."
Z (z): Rarely used in Norwegian and found mostly in loanwords, pronounced like the "s" in "vision" or "ts" in "cats," depending on the word's origin.

The additional letters:

Æ (æ): As mentioned before, similar to the "a" in "cat."
Ø (ø): Similar to the "i" in "bird."
Å (å): As described, akin to the "o" in "more."

Note that the letters 'q', 'w', 'x', 'z' are less common in native Norwegian words and are often found in names, loanwords, and foreign terms. Their pronunciation is typically influenced by the rules of the original language from which the word is borrowed.

Norwegian Intonation and Stress

Norwegian intonation is known for its musicality, setting it apart within the Scandinavian languages. Typically, stress in Norwegian words falls on the first syllable, and it's more about pitch variation than volume.

Common Pronunciation Challenges

Vanskelige Vokalkombinasjoner (Challenging Vowel Sounds)

Norwegian encompasses a wide range of vowel sounds, several of which are not found in English. Mastering these sounds, particularly in combinations, is critical. The distinction between long and short vowels can also be pivotal for the correct interpretation of words.

Tips for Practicing Pronunciation

1. **Lytt Nøye (Listen Carefully):** Engaging with Norwegian media, such as music, podcasts, and watching Norwegian films or TV shows, is an excellent method to familiarize yourself with the language's rhythm and melody.

2. **Gjenta Etter en Innfødt (Repeat After a Native Speaker):** Practicing with native speakers, either in person or through language exchange apps, is invaluable for refining your pronunciation.

3. **Bruk et Speil (Use a Mirror):** Watching your own mouth movements can help ensure that your lips, teeth, and tongue are positioned correctly for producing accurate Norwegian sounds.

4. **Øv Regelmessig (Practice Regularly):** Consistent practice is essential for improvement, even if it's only a few minutes daily.

5. **Vær ikke Redd for å Gjøre Feil (Don't Fear Mistakes):** Embrace errors as they are a fundamental part of the learning process and contribute to better comprehension and skill.

Clear pronunciation is key to immersing yourself in the rich sonic landscape of Norwegian. Embrace the challenge of mastering unique vowels and pitch patterns, and watch as the language unfolds like Norway's vast and varied landscapes. From the crisp clarity of vowels like 'ø' and 'å' to the distinctive sounds of 'kj' and 'skj', each subtlety captures the spirit of Norway's rich history and culture. With dedicated practice and an attentive ear to the rhythmic nuances of Norwegian, your communication will evolve beyond just simple words.

What You'll Find Inside

- **Viktige Uttrykk (Essential Phrases):** A selection of phrases and expressions for various situations you might encounter in Norwegian-speaking environments.

- **Interaktive Øvelser (Interactive Exercises):** Engaging exercises designed to test and improve your language skills and encourage active use of Norwegian.

- **Kulturelle Innsikter (Cultural Insights):** Delve into the vibrant tapestry of Norwegian-speaking regions, from their social customs to historical landmarks.

- **Ytterligere Ressurser (Additional Resources):** A compilation of further materials and advice for deepening your Norwegian language proficiency, including websites, literature recommendations, and travel tips.

How to Use This Phrase Book

This book is carefully designed to support both beginners embarking on their Norwegian language journey and intermediate learners seeking to advance their skills. Begin your linguistic exploration with essential phrases tailored for various situations, ranging from simple greetings to navigating the nuances of Norwegian social customs. As you grow more confident, venture into more intricate language structures and idiomatic expressions that bring you closer to the fluency of a native speaker.

Within these pages, you'll find cultural insights that deepen your connection with Norway's rich history and vibrant contemporary life. Interactive exercises are strategically integrated to reinforce your learning and enable you to incorporate new words and grammar seamlessly into your conversations.

Learning a language is more than memorization; it's an engaging, continuous pursuit of connection. Dive into Norwegian dialogues, engage with Norway's renowned literary works, and embrace the customs that weave the fabric of this unique culture.

Each individual's journey to language mastery is unique, characterized by its own pace and milestones. Nurture your skills with patience, enthusiasm, and an adventurous spirit. With consistent effort, your proficiency and confidence in Norwegian will not just improve; they will flourish.

Klar til å starte? (Ready to start?)

Embark on a rewarding journey into the heart of the Norwegian language and culture. Unravel its linguistic intricacies and immerse yourself in the cultural richness that Norway offers. This adventure promises to be as enriching as it is transformative, broadening your horizons and enhancing your global connections.

GREETINGS & INTRODUCTIONS

- BASIC GREETINGS -
- INTRODUCING YOURSELF AND OTHERS -
- EXPRESSING POLITENESS AND FORMALITY -

Basic Greetings

1. Hi!
   Hei!
   (Hay!)

2. Hello!
   Hallo!
   (Hah-loh!)

   > **Idiomatic Expression:** "Å gå på en smell." -
   > Meaning: "To fail or face a setback."
   > (Literal Translation: "To walk into a bang.")

3. Good morning!
   God morgen!
   (Gohd mohr-gen!)

   > **Cultural Insight:** Norwegians have a deep appreciation
   > for nature, often spending their weekends on "tur" (hikes)
   > regardless of the weather.

4. Good afternoon!
   God ettermiddag!
   (Gohd eht-ter-mee-dahg!)

5. Good evening!
   God kveld!
   (Gohd kveld!)

6. How are you?
   Hvordan har du det? (formal) / Hvordan går det? (informal)
   (Vor-dan har doo deh?) / (Vor-dan gohr deh?)

   > **Cultural Insight:** The concept of 'dugnad' refers to
   > voluntary work done together with others for the
   > community's benefit.

7. Everything good?
   Alt bra?
   (Ahl brah?)

8. How is it going?
   Hvordan går det?
   (Vor-dan gohr deh?)

9. How is everything?
   Hvordan er alt?
   (Vor-dan air ahl?)

10. I'm good, thank you.
    Jeg har det bra, takk.
    (Yai har deh brah, tahk.)

11. And you?
    Og med deg? (formal) / Og du? (informal)
    (Oh meh deh?) / (Oh doo?)

12. Let me introduce...
    La meg introdusere...
    (Lah may in-troh-doo-seh-reh...)

13. This is...
    Dette er...
    (Deh-teh air...)

14. Nice to meet you!
    Hyggelig å møte deg!
    (Hoo-guh-lee oh mø-teh deh!)

15. Delighted!
    Veldig hyggelig!
    (Vehl-dee hoo-guh-lee!)

16. How have you been?
    Hvordan har du hatt det i det siste?
    (Vor-dan har doo haht deh ee deh see-steh?)

Politeness and Formality

17. Excuse me.
    Unnskyld meg.
    (Oon-shool meh.)

18. Please.
    Vær så snill. (formal/informal)
    (Vair soh snill.)

19. Thank you.
    Takk.
    (Tahk.)

> **Fun Fact:** Norway has two official written languages - Bokmål and Nynorsk.

20. Thank you very much!
    Tusen takk!
    (Too-sen tahk!)

21. I'm sorry.
Jeg beklager.
(Yai beh-klah-ger.)

22. I apologize.
Jeg ber om unnskyldning.
(Yai bair ohm oon-shool-neeng.)

23. Sir
Herre
(Heh-reh)

24. Madam
Fru
(Froo)

25. Miss
Frøken
(Fruh-ken)

26. Your name, please?
Hva heter du? (informal) / Hva heter De? (formal)
(Vah heh-ter doo?) / (Vah heh-ter Deh?)

27. Can I help you with anything?
Kan jeg hjelpe deg med noe?
(Kan yai yel-peh deh meh noo-eh?)

28. I am thankful for your help.
Jeg er takknemlig for hjelpen din.
(Yai air takk-nem-lee for yel-pen deen.)

29. The pleasure is mine.
Gleden er på min side.
(Gleh-den air poh meen see-deh.)

30. Thank you for your hospitality.
    Takk for gjestfriheten deres.
    (Tahk for yest-free-heh-ten deh-res.)

31. It's nice to see you again.
    Det er hyggelig å se deg igjen.
    (Deh air hoo-guh-lee oh seh deh ee-yen.)

Greetings for Different Times of Day

32. Good morning, my friend!
    God morgen, min venn!
    (Gohd mohr-gen, meen vehn!)

33. Good afternoon, colleague!
    God ettermiddag, kollega!
    (Gohd eh-tter-mee-dahg, koh-leh-gah!)

34. Good evening neighbor!
    God kveld, nabo!
    (Gohd kveld, nah-boo!)

35. Have a good night!
    God natt!
    (Gohd naht!)

36. Sleep well!
    Sov godt!
    (Sohv goht!)

Special Occasions

37. Happy birthday!
Gratulerer med dagen!
(Gra-too-leh-rer meh dah-gen!)

> **Language Learning Tip:** Don't Fear Mistakes - Making mistakes is a natural part of the learning process.

38. Merry Christmas!
God jul!
(Gohd yool!)

39. Happy Easter!
God påske!
(Gohd pohs-keh!)

> **Travel Story:** At a cozy mountain lodge in Telemark, the host greeted guests with "Velkommen til fjells," meaning "Welcome to the mountains."

40. Happy holidays!
God ferie!
(Gohd feh-ree-eh!)

41. Happy New Year!
Godt nyttår!
(Gohd newt-ohr!)

> **Idiomatic Expression:** "Det er ikke min kopp te." - Meaning: "It's not my cup of tea."
> (Literal Translation: "It's not my cup of tea.")

Meeting Someone for the First Time

42. Pleasure to meet you.
    Hyggelig å møte deg.
    (Hoo-guh-lee oh mø-teh deh.)

> **Language Learning Tip:** Set Realistic Goals - Set
> achievable goals to stay motivated and track your
> progress.

43. I am [Your Name].
    Jeg heter [Ditt Navn].
    (Yai heh-ter [Dit Nahvn].)

44. Where are you from?
    Hvor kommer du fra?
    (Vohr kohm-mer doo frah?)

> **Language Learning Tip:** Join online communities where
> you can practice Norwegian with others.

45. I'm on vacation.
    Jeg er på ferie.
    (Yai air poh feh-ree-eh.)

46. What is your profession?
    Hva jobber du med?
    (Vah yoh-ber doo meh?)

47. How long will you stay here?
Hvor lenge blir du her?
(Vohr lehn-geh bleer doo hair?)

Responding to Greetings

48. Hello, how have you been?
Hallo, hvordan har du hatt det?
(Hah-loh, vor-dan har doo haht deh?)

> **Cultural Insight:** An important aspect of Norwegian culture that emphasizes humility, equality, and the idea that no one is better than anyone else.

49. I've been very busy lately.
Jeg har vært veldig opptatt i det siste.
(Yai har vairt vehl-dee ohp-taht ee deh see-steh.)

50. I've had ups and downs.
Jeg har hatt mine opp- og nedturer.
(Yai har haht meen-eh opp- oh neh-too-rer.)

> **Idiomatic Expression:** "Å bite i det sure eplet." - Meaning: "To accept an unpleasant situation." Literal Translation: "To bite into the sour apple."

51. Thanks for asking.
Takk for at du spør.
(Tahk for aht doo spur.)

52. I feel great.
    Jeg føler meg flott.
    (Yai fuh-ler may floht.)

53. Life has been good.
    Livet har vært bra.
    (Lee-veht har vairt brah.)

54. I can't complain.
    Jeg kan ikke klage.
    (Yai kahn eek-keh klah-geh.)

55. And you, how are you?
    Og du, hvordan har du det?
    (Oh doo, vor-dan har doo deh?)

> **Language Learning Tip:** Practice Daily - Consistency is key in language learning. Even a few minutes each day can make a big difference.

56. I've had some challenges.
    Jeg har hatt noen utfordringer.
    (Yai har haht noo-ehn oot-for-dreen-ger.)

57. Life is a journey.
    Livet er en reise.
    (Lee-veht air en rye-seh.)

58. Thank God, I'm fine.
    Takk Gud, jeg har det bra.
    (Tahk Goo-d, yai har deh brah.)

Informal Greetings

59. What's up?
    Hva skjer?
    (Vah sh-yer?)

60. All good?
    Alt bra?
    (Ahl brah?)

61. Hi, everything okay?
    Hei, er alt bra?
    (Hay, air ahl brah?)

62. I'm good, and you?
    Jeg har det bra, og du?
    (Yai har deh brah, oh doo?)

63. How's life?
    Hvordan er livet?
    (Vor-dan air lee-veht?)

64. Cool!
    Kult!
    (Koolt!)

Saying Goodbye

65. Goodbye!
    Ha det!
    (Hah deh!)

66. See you later!
   Sees senere!
   (Sees seh-neh-reh!)

   Language Learning Tip: Use Flashcards - Create or use online flashcards for vocabulary building.

67. Bye!
   Ha det!
   (Hah deh!)

68. Have a good day.
   Ha en fin dag.
   (Hah en feen dahg.)

   Language Learning Tip: Label Your Surroundings - Put labels in Norwegian on objects around your home.

69. Have a good weekend.
   Ha en god helg.
   (Hah en gohd helg.)

70. Take care.
   Ta vare på deg selv.
   (Tah vah-reh poh deh selv.)

71. Bye, see you later.
   Ha det, sees senere.
   (Hah deh, sees seh-neh-reh.)

72. I need to go now.
   Jeg må gå nå.
   (Yai moh goh noh.)

73. Take care my friend!
    Ta vare på deg selv, min venn!
    (Tah vah-reh poh deh selv, meen vehn!)

Parting Words

74. Hope to see you soon.
    Håper å se deg snart.
    (Hoh-per oh seh deh snart.)

75. Stay in touch.
    Hold kontakten.
    (Hold kon-tahk-ten.)

76. I'll miss you.
    Jeg kommer til å savne deg.
    (Yai kohm-mer til oh sav-neh deh.)

77. Be well.
    Ha det bra.
    (Hah deh brah.)

"Etter regn kommer sol."
"After rain comes sun."
Difficult times are followed by good times.

Interactive Challenge: Greetings Quiz

1. Which Norwegian phrase is a common way to greet people in the morning?

    a) Hva gjør du?
    b) God morgen!
    c) Hvordan har du det?

2. What does the phrase "Hyggelig å møte deg" mean in English?

    a) Excuse me!
    b) Pleased to meet you!
    c) How are you?

3. When is it appropriate to use the phrase "God kveld!"?

    a) In the morning
    b) In the afternoon
    c) In the evening

4. Which phrase is used to ask someone how they are doing in Norwegian?

    a) Takk
    b) Hvordan går det?
    c) Hvor går du?

5. In Norway, when can you use the greeting "Hei!"?

    a) Only in the morning
    b) Only in the afternoon
    c) Anytime

6. **What is the Norwegian equivalent of "And you?"?**

    a) Og du?
    b) Takk
    c) Hva gjør du?

7. **When expressing gratitude in Norwegian, what do you say?**

    a) Unnskyld
    b) Hyggelig å møte deg
    c) Takk

8. **How do you say "Excuse me" in Norwegian?**

    a) Unnskyld meg
    b) God ettermiddag!
    c) Alt er bra?

9. **Which phrase is used to inquire about someone's well-being?**

    a) Hvor bor du?
    b) Hvordan går det?
    c) Takk

10. **In a typical Norwegian conversation, when is it common to ask about someone's background and interests during a first-time meeting?**

    a) Never
    b) Only in formal situations
    c) Always

11. In Norwegian, what does "Hyggelig å møte deg" mean?

a) Delighted to meet you
b) Excuse me
c) Thank you

12. When should you use the phrase "Hvordan går det?"?

a) When ordering food
b) When asking for directions
c) When inquiring about someone's well-being

13. Which phrase is used to make requests politely?

a) Hvordan går det?
b) Hva vil du ha?
c) Vær så snill

14. What is the equivalent of "I'm sorry" in Norwegian?

a) Beklager
b) Hvordan går det?
c) Alt er i orden?

Correct Answers:

1. b)
2. b)
3. c)
4. b)
5. c)
6. a)
7. c)
8. a)
9. b)
10. c)
11. a)
12. c)
13. c)
14. a)

EATING & DINING

- ORDERING FOOD AND DRINKS IN A RESTAURANT -
- DIETARY PREFERENCES AND RESTRICTIONS -
- COMPLIMENTS AND COMPLAINTS ABOUT FOOD -

Basic Ordering

78. I'd like a table for two, please.
    Jeg vil gjerne ha et bord for to, takk.
    (Yai vil yarn-eh hah eht bohrd for toh, tahk.)

79. What's the special of the day?
    Hva er dagens spesial?
    (Vah air dah-gens speh-see-ahl?)

> **Cultural Insight:** Being on time is highly valued in Norwegian culture, reflecting respect and efficiency.

80. Can I see the menu, please?
    Kan jeg se menyen, vær så snill?
    (Kan yai seh meh-nyen, vair soh snill?)

81. I'll have the steak, medium rare.
    Jeg tar biffen, medium stekt.
    (Yai tahr bif-fen, meh-dee-oom stekt.)

82. Can I get a glass of water?
    Kan jeg få et glass vann?
    (Kan yai foh eht glahss vann?)

> **Travel Story:** On a train journey through the snowy landscapes, a passenger shared his love for winter with "Norsk vinter er som et eventyr," meaning "Norwegian winter is like a fairy tale."

83. Can you bring us some bread to start?
Kan du bringe oss litt brød for å starte?
(Kan doo breeng-eh oss leet bruhd for oh start-eh?)

84. Do you have a vegetarian option?
Har dere et vegetarisk alternativ?
(Har deh-reh eht veh-geh-tah-risk ahl-ter-nah-teev?)

> **Language Learning Tip:** Listen to Norwegian Music - Music can be a fun way to learn new words and improve pronunciation.

85. Is there a kids' menu available?
Har dere en barnemeny?
(Har deh-reh ehn bar-neh-meh-nee?)

86. We'd like to order appetizers to share.
Vi vil gjerne bestille forretter å dele.
(Vee vil yarn-eh behs-teel-leh fohr-reht-ter oh deh-leh.)

87. Can we have separate checks, please?
Kan vi få separate regninger, takk?
(Kan vee foh seh-pah-rah-teh rehg-neen-ger, tahk?)

88. Could you recommend a vegetarian dish?
Kan du anbefale en vegetarisk rett?
(Kan doo ahn-beh-fah-leh ehn veh-geh-tah-risk rehtt?)

89. I'd like to try the local cuisine.
Jeg vil gjerne prøve det lokale kjøkkenet.
(Yai vil yarn-eh pruh-veh deht loh-kah-leh yuh-keh-neht.)

90. May I have a refill on my drink, please?
   Kan jeg få påfyll på drikken min, takk?
   (Kan yai foh poh-fill poh dreek-ken meen, tahk?)

> **Language Learning Tip:** Watch Norwegian TV Shows and Movies - This helps in understanding conversational language and cultural context.

91. What's the chef's special today?
   Hva er kokkens spesial i dag?
   (Vah air kohk-kens speh-see-ahl ee dahg?)

92. Can you make it extra spicy?
   Kan du gjøre den ekstra krydret?
   (Kan doo yur-reh dehn ehk-strah kree-dret?)

93. I'll have the chef's tasting menu.
   Jeg tar kokkens smaksmeny.
   (Yai tahr kohk-kens smahks-meh-nee.)

Special Requests

94. I'm allergic to nuts. Is this dish nut-free?
   Jeg er allergisk mot nøtter. Er denne retten uten nøtter?
   (Yai air ah-ler-gisk moht nuht-ter. Air dehn-neh reh-ten ooh-ten nuht-ter?)

95. I'm on a gluten-free diet. What can I have?
   Jeg er på en glutenfri diett. Hva kan jeg bestille?
   (Yai air poh ehn gloo-ten-free dee-ett. Vah kahn yai behs-teel-leh?)

96. Can you make it less spicy, please?
Kan du gjøre den mindre krydret, takk?
(Kan doo yur-reh dehn meen-dreh kree-dret, tahk?)

> **Idiomatic Expression:** "Å være midt i blinken." -
> Meaning: "To be exactly right."
> (Literal translation: "To be right in the bullseye.")

97. Can you recommend a local specialty?
Kan du anbefale en lokal spesialitet?
(Kan doo ahn-beh-fah-leh ehn loh-kahl speh-see-ahl-ee-teht?)

98. Could I have my salad without onions?
Kan jeg få salaten min uten løk?
(Kan yai foh sah-lah-ten meen ooh-ten lurk?)

99. Are there any daily specials?
Har dere noen dagens tilbud?
(Har deh-reh noo-ehn dah-gens teel-bood?)

> **Fun Fact:** Norway is known for its stunning fjords, deep
> coastal inlets carved by glacial activity.

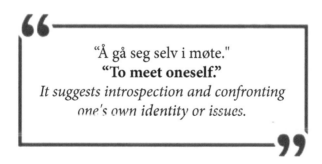

"Å gå seg selv i møte."
"To meet oneself."
*It suggests introspection and confronting
one's own identity or issues.*

100.   Can I get a side of extra sauce?
Kan jeg få litt ekstra saus?
(Kan yai foh lit ehk-strah sowss?)

101.   I'd like a glass of red/white wine, please.
Jeg vil gjerne ha et glass rød/hvit vin, takk.
(Yai vil yarn-eh hah eht glahss ruhd/hveet veen, tahk.)

102.   Could you bring the bill, please?
Kan du ta med regningen, vær så snill?
(Kan doo tah meh rehg-neen-gen, vair soh snill?)

Allergies and Intolerances

103.   I have a dairy allergy. Is the sauce dairy-free?
Jeg er allergisk mot melkeprodukter. Er sausen uten melk?
(Yai air ah-lehr-gisk moht mel-keh-proh-dook-ter. Air sow-sen oo-ten melk?)

> **Fun Fact:** In Northern Norway, the sun doesn't set for about two months in summer, creating the phenomenon of the Midnight Sun.

104.   Does this contain any seafood? I have an allergy.
Inneholder dette sjømat? Jeg er allergisk.
(Een-neh-hohl-der deht-teh shuh-maht? Yai air ah-lehr-gisk.)

105.   I can't eat anything with soy. Is that an issue?
Jeg kan ikke spise noe med soya. Er det et problem?
(Yai kahn eek-keh spee-seh noo-eh meh soh-yah. Air deht eht proh-blem?)

106. I'm lactose intolerant, so no dairy, please.
Jeg er laktoseintolerant, så ingen melkeprodukter, takk.
(Yai air lahk-toh-seh-een-toh-leh-rant, soh een-gen mel-keh-proh-dook-ter, tahk.)

107. Is there an option for those with nut allergies?
Finnes det et alternativ for de med nøtteallergi?
(Fee-nes deht eht ahl-tehr-nah-teev for deh meh nuht-teh-ahl-lehr-gee?)

108. I'm following a vegan diet. Is that possible?
Jeg følger en vegansk diett. Er det mulig?
(Yai fuhl-ger ehn veh-gahn-sk dee-ett. Air deht moo-leeg?)

> **Cultural Insight:** Norway is one of the world's top coffee consumers per capita, and coffee breaks are a cherished part of daily life.

109. Is this dish suitable for someone with allergies?
Er denne retten egnet for noen med allergier?
(Air dehn-neh reh-ten ehg-neht for noo-ehn meh ah-lehr-gee-er?)

110. I'm trying to avoid dairy. Any dairy-free options?
Jeg prøver å unngå melkeprodukter. Finnes det melkefrie alternativer?
(Yai pruh-ver oh oon-goh mel-keh-proh-dook-ter. Fee-nes deht mel-keh-free ah-ltehr-nah-tee-ver?)

111. I have a shellfish allergy. Is it safe to order seafood?
Jeg er allergisk mot skalldyr. Er det trygt å bestille sjømat?
(Yai air ah-lehr-gisk moht shahl-deer. Air deht trygt oh bch stcel-leh shuh-maht?)

112.   Can you make this gluten-free?
       Kan dere lage dette glutenfritt?
       (Kan deh-reh lah-geh deh-teh gloo-ten-freet?)

> **Language Learning Tip:** Record Yourself Speaking -
> This can help in self-assessment and improve your
> pronunciation.

Specific Dietary Requests

113.   I prefer my food without cilantro.
       Jeg foretrekker maten min uten koriander.
       (Yai foh-reh-trek-ker mah-ten meen oo-ten koh-ree-ahn-der.)

114.   Could I have the dressing on the side?
       Kan jeg få dressingen ved siden av?
       (Kan yai foh dreh-sing-en vehd see-den ahv?)

115.   Can you make it vegan-friendly?
       Kan dere lage den vegansk?
       (Kan deh-reh lah-geh dehn veh-gahn-sk?)

116.   I'd like extra vegetables with my main course.
       Jeg vil gjerne ha ekstra grønnsaker til hovedretten.
       *(Yai vil yarn-eh hah ehk-strah gruhn-sah-ker teel
       hoh-veh-reht-ten.)*

117.   Is this suitable for someone on a keto diet?
       Er dette egnet for noen på en keto diett?
       (Air deh-teh ehg-neht for noo-ehn poh en keh-toh dee-ett?)

118.   I prefer my food with less oil, please.
Jeg foretrekker maten min med mindre olje, takk.
(Yai foh-reh-trek-ker mah-ten meen meh meen-dreh ol-yeh, tahk.)

119.   Is this dish suitable for vegetarians?
Er denne retten egnet for vegetarianere?
(Air dehn-neh reh-ten ehg-neht for veh-geh-tah-ree-ah-neh-reh?)

120.   I'm on a low-carb diet. What would you recommend?
Jeg er på en lavkarbo diett. Hva vil dere anbefale?
(Yai air poh en lahv-kahr-boh dee-ett. Vah vil deh-reh ahn-beh-fah-leh?)

> **Fun Fact:** The Nobel Peace Prize is awarded in Oslo, Norway, every year.

121.   Is the bread here gluten-free?
Er brødet her glutenfritt?
(Air bruh-deht hair gloo-ten-freet?)

122.   I'm watching my sugar intake. Any sugar-free desserts?
Jeg passer på sukkerinntaket mitt. Har dere sukkerfrie desserter?
(Yai pah-ser poh sook-ker-een-tah-keht meett. Har deh-reh sook-ker-free deh-sehr-tehr?)

> **Travel Story:** In Bergen, at the bustling Fish Market, a fishmonger described their freshest catch with "Fersk som fisken," meaning "Fresh as the fish."

Compliments

123. This meal is delicious!
Dette måltidet er deilig!
(Deh-teh mohl-tee-deh air deh-leeg!)

> **Fun Fact:** Besides Norwegian, the indigenous Sami people in Norway speak their own languages, which are officially recognized.

124. The flavors in this dish are amazing.
Smakene i denne retten er utrolige.
(Smaah-keh-neh ee dehn-neh reh-ten air ooh-troh-lee-geh.)

125. I love the presentation of the food.
Jeg elsker presentasjonen av maten.
(Yai ehl-sker preh-sen-tah-sjooh-nen ahv mah-ten.)

126. This dessert is outstanding!
Denne desserten er fantastisk!
(Dehn-neh deh-sehr-ten air fan-tas-tisk!)

127. The service here is exceptional.
Servicen her er eksepsjonell.
(Sehr-vee-sehn hair air ehk-sehp-syooh-nehl.)

> **Language Learning Tip:** Translate Your Favorite Songs - This can help in expanding vocabulary and understanding nuances.

128. The chef deserves praise for this dish.
Kokken fortjener ros for denne retten.
(Kohk-ken for-tyeh-ner rohs for dehn-neh reh-ten.)

129. I'm impressed by the quality of the ingredients.
Jeg er imponert over kvaliteten på ingrediensene.
(Yai air eem-poh-nehr oh-vehr kval-ee-teh-ten poh een-greh-dyen-seh-neh.)

130. The atmosphere in this restaurant is wonderful.
Atmosfæren i denne restauranten er fantastisk.
(At-mohs-fay-ren ee dehn-neh res-tau-rahnten air fan-tas-tisk.)

131. Everything we ordered was perfect.
Alt vi bestilte var perfekt.
(Ahl vee behs-teel-teh vahr per-fekt.)

Compaints

132. The food is cold. Can you reheat it?
Maten er kald. Kan dere varme den opp igjen?
(Mah-ten air kahld. Kan deh-reh vahr-meh dehn ohp eeg-yen?)

> **Fun Fact:** Norway is one of the best places to witness the Aurora Borealis, or Northern Lights.

133. This dish is too spicy for me.
Denne retten er for sterk for meg.
(Dehn-neh reh-ten air for ster-keh for may.)

134. The portion size is quite small.
Porsjonsstørrelsen er ganske liten.
(Por-shohn-stuh-rel-sehn air gahn-skeh lee-ten.)

135. There's a hair in my food.
    Det er et hår i maten min.
    (Deh air eht hohr ee mah-ten meen.)

136. I'm not satisfied with the service.
    Jeg er ikke fornøyd med servicen.
    (Yai air eek-keh for-nurd meh sehr-vee-sehn.)

137. The soup is lukewarm.
    Suppen er lunken.
    (Soop-pen air loon-ken.)

138. The sauce on this dish is too salty.
    Sausen på denne retten er for salt.
    (Sow-sen poh dehn-neh reh-ten air for sahlt.)

    > **Idiomatic Expression:** "Å kaste perler for svin."
    > Meaning: "To waste something valuable on someone who doesn't appreciate it."
    > (Literal translation: "To throw pearls for swine.")

139. The dessert was a bit disappointing.
    Desserten var litt skuffende.
    (Deh-sehr-ten vahr leet skoof-fen-deh.)

140. I ordered this dish, but you brought me something else.
    Jeg bestilte denne retten, men dere ga meg noe annet.
    (Yai behs-teel-teh dehn-neh reh-ten, mehn deh-reh gah may noo-eh ahn-net.)

141. The food took a long time to arrive.
    Maten tok lang tid å komme.
    (Mah-ten took lahng teed oh kohm-meh.)

Specific Dish Feedback

142. The steak is overcooked.
    Biffen er overstekt.
    (Bif-fen air oh-ver-stekt.)

> **Fun Fact:** Norway was home to the Vikings, renowned seafarers from the late 8th to early 11th centuries.

143. This pasta is undercooked.
    Denne pastaen er underkokt.
    (Dehn-neh pah-stah-en air oon-der-kohkt.)

144. The fish tastes off. Is it fresh?
    Fisken smaker rart. Er den fersk?
    (Fis-ken smah-ker raart. Air dehn fehrsk?)

145. The salad dressing is too sweet.
    Dressingen til salaten er for søt.
    (Dreh-sing-en teel sah-lah-ten air for sert.)

146. The rice is underseasoned.
    Risen er underkrydret.
    (Ree-sen air oon-der-kree-dret.)

> **Language Learning Tip:** Learn About Norwegian History - This can provide insight into the language's evolution.

147. The dessert lacks flavor.
    Desserten mangler smak.
    (Deh-sehr-ten mahn-gler smahk.)

148. The vegetables are overcooked.
Grønnsakene er overkokt.
(Groon-sah-keh-neh air oh-ver-kohkt.)

149. The pizza crust is burnt.
Pizzabunnen er brent.
(Pee-tsah-boon-nehn air brent.)

> **Travel Story:** Atop the snowy slopes of Lillehammer, a ski instructor encouraged a hesitant skier with "Bare hyggelig!" meaning "Just pleasant!" or "Don't worry about it!"

150. The burger is dry.
Burgeren er tørr.
(Boor-gehr-en air turr.)

151. The fries are too greasy.
Pommes frites er for fete.
(Pohm freet-es air for feh-teh.)

152. The soup is too watery.
Suppen er for vannaktig.
(Soop-pen air for vahn-ahk-tee.)

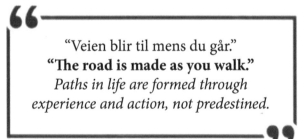

"Veien blir til mens du går."
"The road is made as you walk."
Paths in life are formed through experience and action, not predestined.

Word Search Puzzle: Eating & Dining

RESTAURANT
RESTAURANT
MENU
MENY
APPETIZER
FORRETT
VEGETARIAN
VEGETARIANER
ALLERGY
ALLERGI
VEGAN
VEGANER
SPECIAL
SPESIAL
DESSERT
DESSERT
SERVICE
SERVICE
CHEF
SJEFKOKK
INGREDIENTS
INGREDIENSER
ATMOSPHERE
ATMOSFÆRE
PERFECT
PERFEKT

```
U K L G T N S T H L V J V S I
I S Q X A N U B X K G B A P N
V I H G T S A T U Z L T L E G
Y S E U L O Z R H W M A H S R
A V P F V W E G U O N T J I E
E P M E E M R G S A P Q H A D
V C P C C R U P S F T M T L I
Z Q I E A I H H Q O A S V I E
L A M V T E A J H R D E E G N
G E Z F R I D L G R G Y T R S
I J N E Q E Z Z J E P S K E E
R N S P S L S E T T P U E L R
K X G S R F A A R T Q W F L P
A F E R L H R H S K G F R A H
J R L A E I Y G P G E C E X O
T Y T V A D P O U H G E P K Q
Y D M N M W I N C S W C A N F
Y J X N M Y E E H W Z I L V X
W A Q W G M G H N R I V Z J T
S J E F K O K K Y T A R S Q P
T R E S S E D B A G S E M R T
E R Æ F S O M T A U R S L X N
B O Q M E N Y L F L F E U W A
R E N A I R A T E G E V L J R
O S Y Z T S I W C A J S L L U
W X C U H F T S Z E C E J E A
I N Q E C P P U D U F W J D T
H D E V L T Z N W L N R E U S
F J Y R C R W Y M X H K E L E
D V E G A N E R L M A Y U P R
```

Correct Answers:

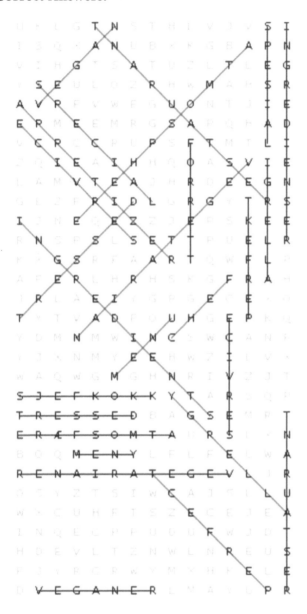

TRAVEL & TRANSPORTATION

- ASKING FOR DIRECTIONS -
- BUYING TICKETS FOR TRANSPORTATION -
- INQUIRING ABOUT TRAVEL-RELATED INFORMATION -

Directions

153.   How do I get to the nearest bus stop?
Hvordan kommer jeg til nærmeste bussholdeplass?
(Vor-dan kohm-mer yai teel nair-mehs-teh boosh-hol-deh-plahss?)

> **Fun Fact:** Norway is one of the world's largest oil exporters and has a very high standard of living due to its oil wealth.

154.   Can you show me the way to the train station?
Kan du vise meg veien til togstasjonen?
(Kan doo vee-seh may vee-ehn teel tohg-stah-shoh-nen?)

155.   Is there a map of the city center?
Finnes det et kart over sentrum?
(Fee-nes deht eht kahrt oh-ver sen-troom?)

156.   Which street leads to the airport?
Hvilken gate fører til flyplassen?
(Vil-ken gah-teh fur-er teel flee-plah-sen?)

157.   Where is the nearest taxi stand?
Hvor er nærmeste taxiholdeplass?
(Vohr air nair-mehs-teh tak-see-hol-deh-plahss?)

> **Travel Story:** In the heart of Oslo, a local pointed out the way to the Munch Museum with "Rett frem og til høyre," meaning "Straight ahead and to the right."

158. How can I find the hotel from here?
Hvordan finner jeg hotellet herfra?
(Vor-dan feen-ner yai ho-teh-lett hair-frah?)

> **Fun Fact:** Norway has one of the longest coastlines in the world, stretching over 25,000 kilometers.

159. What's the quickest route to the museum?
Hva er den raskeste ruten til museet?
(Vah air dehn rahs-keh-steh roo-ten teel moo-see-eht?)

160. Is there a pedestrian path to the beach?
Finnes det en gangsti til stranden?
(Fee-nes deht ehn gahng-stee teel strahn-den?)

161. Can you point me towards the city square?
Kan du peke meg mot bytorget?
(Kan doo peh-keh may moht bee-tor-geht?)

> **Idiomatic Expression:** "Å sette fingeren på noe." - Meaning: "To pinpoint something."
> (Literal translation: "To put the finger on something.")

162. How do I find the trailhead for the hiking trail?
Hvordan finner jeg startpunktet for turstien?
(Vor-dan feen-ner yai start-poonk-teht for toor-stee-en?)

> **Fun Fact:** Norway's currency is the Krone, which means "crown" in Norwegian.

Ticket Purchase

163. How much is a one-way ticket to downtown?
      Hvor mye koster en enveisbillett til sentrum?
      (Vohr mee-eh kohs-ter en en-vise-bee-lett teel sen-troom?)

164. Are there any discounts for students?
      Er det studentrabatter?
      (Air deht stoo-den-trah-bah-ter?)

      Language Learning Tip: Follow Norwegian language
      accounts on platforms like Instagram or Twitter.

165. What's the price of a monthly bus pass?
      Hva koster et månedskort for bussen?
      (Vah kohs-ter eht moh-nehs-kohrt for boo-sen?)

166. Can I buy a metro ticket for a week?
      Kan jeg kjøpe en ukesbillett til metroen?
      (Kan yai shuh-peh en oo-kes-bee-lett teel meh-troh-en?)

167. How do I get a refund for a canceled flight?
      Hvordan får jeg refusjon for en kansellert flyvning?
      (Vor-dan for yai reh-foo-sjoon for en kahn-seh-lert fleev-ning?)

      Fun Fact: Norway has over 1,000 road tunnels, including
      some of the world's longest and deepest.

168. Is it cheaper to purchase tickets online or at the station?
Er det billigere å kjøpe billetter på nett eller på stasjonen?
(Air deht bee-lee-geh-reh oh shuh-peh bee-leht-ter poh net eh-ler poh stah-sjooh-nen?)

169. Can I upgrade my bus ticket to first class?
Kan jeg oppgradere bussbilletten min til første klasse?
(Kan yai ohp-grah-deh-reh booss-bee-leht-ten meen teel fur-steh klahs-seh?)

170. Are there any promotions for weekend train travel?
Finnes det tilbud for togreiser i helgene?
(Fee-nes deht teel-bood for toh-geye-ser ee hel-geh-neh?)

171. Is there a night bus to the city center?
Er det en nattbuss til sentrum?
(Air deht en naht-booss teel sen-troom?)

> **Idiomatic Expression:** "Å holde tunga rett i munnen." - Meaning: "To be careful or precise in your actions." (Literal translation: "To keep one's tongue straight in the mouth.")

172. What's the cost of a one-day tram pass?
Hva koster et dagskort for trikken?
(Vah kohs-ter eht dahgs-kohrt for treek-ken?)

> **Fun Fact:** Notable Norwegian authors include Henrik Ibsen, one of the founders of Modernism in theatre, and Jo Nesbø, a bestselling crime novelist.

Travel Info

173.   What's the weather forecast for tomorrow?
Hva er værmeldingen for i morgen?
(Vah air vair-mel-deen-gen for ee mohr-gen?)

> **Fun Fact:** The Svalbard archipelago, part of Norway, is one of the few places in the world where you can see polar bears in the wild.

174.   Are there any guided tours of the historical sites?
Finnes det guidede turer av historiske steder?
(Fee-nes deht gee-deh-deh too-rehr ahv hee-stoh-rees-keh steh-der?)

175.   Can you recommend a good local restaurant for dinner?
Kan du anbefale en god lokal restaurant til middag?
(Kan doo ahn-beh-fah-leh en gohd loh-kahl res-tau-rant teel meed-dahg?)

176.   How do I get to the famous landmarks in town?
Hvordan kommer jeg til de berømte landemerkene i byen?
(Vor-dan kohm-mer yai teel deh beh-røm-teh lan-deh-mehr-keh-neh ee bee-ehn?)

177.   Is there a visitor center at the airport?
Er det et besøkssenter på flyplassen?
(Air deht eht beh-suhks-sen-ter poh flee-plahs-sen?)

178.   What's the policy for bringing pets on the train?
Hva er reglene for å ha med kjæledyr på toget?
(Vah air reh-gleh-neh for oh hah meh yæ-leh-dür poh toh-geht?)

179. Are there any discounts for disabled travelers?
Er det rabatter for funksjonshemmede reisende?
(Air deht rah-baht-ter for foonk-shohns-hem-meh-deh rye-sen-deh?)

> **Idiomatic Expression:** "Det er ugler i mosen." - Meaning: "Something is suspicious."
> (Literal translation: "There are owls in the bog.")

180. Can you provide information about local festivals?
Kan dere gi informasjon om lokale festivaler?
(Kan deh-reh gee een-for-mah-sjoon ohm loh-kah-leh fes-tih-vah-ler?)

181. Is there Wi-Fi available on long bus journeys?
Er det Wi-Fi tilgjengelig på lange bussturer?
(Air deht wee-fee teel-yeng-eh-lee poh lahn-geh booss-too-rehr?)

> **Fun Fact:** Norway consistently ranks high in global happiness and quality of life indexes.

182. Where can I rent a bicycle for exploring the city?
Hvor kan jeg leie en sykkel for å utforske byen?
(Vohr kan yai lyeh en seek-kel for oh oot-for-skeh bee-ehn?)

> **Travel Story:** On a leisurely walk in the Vigeland Sculpture Park in Oslo, a passerby commented, "Kunst i hver krok," meaning "Art in every corner."

Getting Around by Public Transportation

183. Which bus should I take to reach the city center?
Hvilken buss skal jeg ta for å komme til sentrum?
(Vil-ken booss skal yai tah for oh kohm-meh teel sen-troom?)

184. Can I buy a day pass for unlimited rides?
Kan jeg kjøpe et dagskort for ubegrensede turer?
(Kan yai shuh-peh eht dahgs-kohrt for oo-beh-gren-seh-deh too-rehr?)

185. Is there a metro station within walking distance?
Er det en t-banestasjon i gangavstand?
(Air deht en teh-bah-neh-stah-shoon ee gahng-ahv-stahnd?)

186. How do I transfer between different bus lines?
Hvordan bytter jeg mellom forskjellige busslinjer?
(Vor-dan bee-tter yai meh-loom for-shjel-lee-geh booss-leen-yehr?)

187. Are there any discounts for senior citizens?
Er det rabatter for pensjonister?
(Air deht rah-baht-ter for pen-shoh-nees-ter?)

188. What's the last bus/train for the night?
Hva er siste buss/tog for natten?
(Vah air see-steh booss/tohg for naht-ten?)

189. Can you recommend a reliable taxi service?
Kan du anbefale en pålitelig taxitjeneste?
(Kan doo ahn-beh-fah-leh en poh-lee-teh-leeg tak-see-tyeh-nes-teh?)

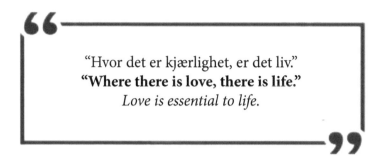

> "Hvor det er kjærlighet, er det liv."
> **"Where there is love, there is life."**
> *Love is essential to life.*

190. Do trams run on weekends as well?
Går trikkene også i helgene?
(Gohr treek-keh-neh oh-gsoh ee hel-geh-neh?)

> **Fun Fact:** Norwegian Magnus Carlsen is a world-renowned chess grandmaster and former world chess champion.

191. Are there any express buses to [destination]?
Finnes det ekspressbusser til [destinasjon]?
(Fee-nes deht ehks-press-boos-ser teel [dehs-tee-nah-shoon]?)

192. What's the fare for a one-way ticket to the suburbs?
Hva koster en enveisbillett til forstedene?
(Vah kohs-ter en en-vise-bee-lett teel for-steh-deh-neh?)

> **Travel Story:** On a scenic fjord cruise in Geirangerfjord, the captain remarked, "Som å seile på et speil," meaning "Like sailing on a mirror," to describe the still waters.

Navigating the Airport

193. Where can I locate the baggage claim area?
Hvor finner jeg bagasjeutleveringsområdet?
(Vohr feen-ner yai bah-gah-sheh-oot-leh-veh-reengs-ohm-roh-det?)

194. Is there a currency exchange counter in the terminal?
Er det en valutavekslingsdisk i terminalen?
(Air deht en vah-loo-tah-vehk-slings-disk ee ter-mee-nah-len?)

> **Idiomatic Expression:** "Å være på bærtur." -
> Meaning: "To be mistaken."
> (Literal translation: "To be on a berry trip.")

195. Are there any pet relief areas for service animals?
Finnes det hvileområder for servicedyr?
(Fee-nes deht vee-leh-ohm-roh-der for ser-vee-seh-deer?)

196. How early can I go through security?
Hvor tidlig kan jeg gå gjennom sikkerhetskontrollen?
(Vohr tee-leeg kan yai goh yoh-noom sik-ker-hets-kohn-trohl-len?)

197. What's the procedure for boarding the aircraft?
Hva er prosedyren for ombordstigning på flyet?
(Vah air proh-seh-dee-ren for ohm-bor-stig-ning poh flee-yet?)

198. Can I use mobile boarding passes?
Kan jeg bruke mobile boardingpass?
(Kan yai broo-keh moh-bee-leh boar-ding-pass?)

199. Are there any restaurants past security?
Er det noen restauranter etter sikkerhetskontrollen?
(Air deht noo-en res-tow-ran-ter eh-ter sik-ker-hets-kohn-trohl-len?)

200. What's the airport's Wi-Fi password?
Hva er Wi-Fi-passordet til flyplassen?
(Vah air Wee-Fee pass-or-det teel flee-plahs-sen?)

201. Can I bring duty-free items on board?
Kan jeg ta med taxfree-varer ombord?
(Kan yai tah meh tak-free vah-rer ohm-bor?)

202. Is there a pharmacy at the airport?
Er det et apotek på flyplassen?
(Air deht eht ah-poh-tek poh flee-plahs-sen?)

Traveling by Car

203. How do I pay tolls on the highway?
Hvordan betaler jeg bompenger på motorveien?
(Vor-dan beh-tah-ler yai bom-pen-ger poh moh-tor-vye-en?)

204. Where can I find a car wash nearby?
Hvor kan jeg finne en bilvask i nærheten?
(Vohr kan yai feen-neh en beel-vahsk ee nair-heh-ten?)

205. Are there electric vehicle charging stations?
Finnes det ladestasjoner for elektriske kjøretøy?
(Fee-nes deht lah-deh-stah-sho-ner for eh-lehk-trees-keh shur-reh-toy?)

206. Can I rent a GPS navigation system with the car?
Kan jeg leie et GPS-navigasjonssystem med bilen?
(Kan yai lyeh eht Jee-Pee-Ess nah-vee-gah-shohns-sys-tehm meh bee-len?)

207. What's the cost of parking in the city center?
Hva koster parkering i sentrum?
(Vah kohs-ter pahr-keh-ring ee sen-troom?)

208. Do I need an international driving permit?
Trenger jeg et internasjonalt førerkort?
(Tren-ger yai eht een-ter-nah-syo-nahl fuhr-ehr-kohrt?)

209. Is roadside assistance available?
Er veihjelp tilgjengelig?
(Air vye-help teel-yeng-eh-lee?)

> **Fun Fact:** Jostedalsbreen in Norway is the largest glacier in continental Europe.

210. Are there any traffic cameras on this route?
Er det trafikkameraer på denne ruten?
(Air deht trah-feek-kahm-eh-rehr poh dehn-neh roo-ten?)

211. Can you recommend a reliable mechanic?
Kan du anbefale en pålitelig mekaniker?
(Kan doo ahn-beh-fah-leh en poh-lee-teh-leeg meh-kah-nee-ker?)

212. What's the speed limit in residential areas?
Hva er fartsgrensen i boligområder?
(Vah air fahrts-gren-sen ee boh-lee-gohm-roh-der?)

Airport Transfers and Shuttles

213. Where is the taxi stand located at the airport?
Hvor er taxiholdeplassen på flyplassen?
(Vohr air tak-see-hol-deh-plahs-sen poh flee-plahs-sen?)

214. Do airport shuttles run 24/7?
Går flyplasstransporten døgnet rundt?
(Gohr flee-plahss-trahn-spor-ten dug-neht roondt?)

> **Idiomatic Expression:** "Å ha mange jern i ilden." -
> Meaning: "To be involved in many activities."
> (Literal translation: "To have many irons in the fire.")

215. How long does it take to reach downtown by taxi?
Hvor lang tid tar det å komme til sentrum med taxi?
(Vohr lahng teed tahr deht oh kohm-meh teel sen-troom meh tak-see?)

216. Is there a designated pick-up area for ride-sharing services?
Er det et eget henteområde for samkjøringstjenester?
(Air deht eht eh-get hen-teh-ohm-roh-deh for sahm-shur-ring-styen-ehs-ter?)

217. Can I book a shuttle in advance?
Kan jeg bestille en shuttle på forhånd?
(Kan yai beh-stee-leh en shuttle poh for-hohnd?)

> **Fun Fact:** Norwegian is a tonal language, where the tone can change the meaning of a word.

218. Do hotels offer free shuttle service to the airport?
Tilbyr hotellene gratis shuttle-service til flyplassen?
(Till-beer ho-tehl-leh-neh grah-tis shut-le ser-vee-seh teel flee-plahs-sen?)

219. What's the rate for a private airport transfer?
Hva er prisen for en privat flyplasstransport?
(Vah air pree-sen for en pree-vat flee-plahss-trahn-sport?)

220. Are there any public buses connecting to the airport?
Er det offentlige busser som går til flyplassen?
(Air deht oh-fen-tlee-geh boo-ser sohm gohr teel flee-plahs-sen?)

221. Can you recommend a reliable limousine service?
Kan du anbefale en pålitelig limousintjeneste?
(Kan doo ahn-beh-fah-leh en poh-lee-teh-leeg lee-moo-seen-tyeh-nes-teh?)

222. Is there an airport shuttle for early morning flights?
Finnes det en flyplasstransport for tidlige morgenflyvninger?
(Fee-nes deht en flee-plahss-trahn-sport for tee-lee-geh mohr-gen-fleev-nee-nger?)

Traveling with Luggage

223. Can I check my bags at this train station?
Kan jeg sjekke inn bagasjen min på denne togstasjonen?
(Kan yai shek-keh een bah-gah-syen meen poh dehn-neh tohg-stah-shoh-nen?)

224. Where can I find baggage carts in the airport?
Hvor kan jeg finne bagasjevogner på flyplassen?
(Vohr kan yai feen-neh bah-gah-sheh-vohg-ner poh flee-plahs-sen?)

> Fun Fact: The Lofoten Islands are known for their dramatic scenery and are a popular tourist destination.

225. Are there weight limits for checked baggage?
Er det vektbegrensninger for innsjekket bagasje?
(Air deht vehkt-beh-gren-snee-nger for eens-shek-keh bah-gah-sheh?)

226. Can I carry my backpack as a personal item?
Kan jeg ta med ryggsekken min som en personlig gjenstand?
(Kan yai tah meh rygg-sehk-ken meen sohm en pehr-soh-ne-lee yen-stahnd?)

227. What's the procedure for oversized luggage?
Hva er prosedyren for overdimensjonert bagasje?
(Vah air proh-seh-dee-ren for oh-ver-dee-mehn-syo-nehrt bah-gah-sheh?)

228. Can I bring a stroller on the bus?
Kan jeg ta med en barnevogn på bussen?
(Kan yai tah meh en bar-ne-vohn poh boo-sen?)

229. Are there lockers for storing luggage at the airport?
Finnes det skap for oppbevaring av bagasje på flyplassen?
(Fee-nes deht skahp for opp-beh-vah-reeng ahv bah-gah-sheh poh flee-plahs-sen?)

> Fun Fact: Norway is home to a large population of moose and reindeer.

230. How do I label my luggage with contact information?
Hvordan merker jeg bagasjen min med kontaktinformasjon?
(Vor-dan mer-ker yai bah-gah-syen meen meh kohn-tahkt-een-for-mah-shoon?)

231. Is there a lost and found office at the train station?
Finnes det et hittegodskontor på togstasjonen?
(Fee-nes deht eht heet-teh-gohds-kohn-tohr poh tohg-stah-shoh-nen?)

> **Idiomatic Expression:** "Å være ute å kjøre." -
> Meaning: "To be completely wrong."
> (Literal translation: "To be out driving.")

232. Can I carry fragile items in my checked bags?
Kan jeg ta med skjøre gjenstander i innsjekket bagasje?
(Kan yai tah meh shjø-reh yen-stahn-der ee eens-shek-keh bah-gah-sheh?)

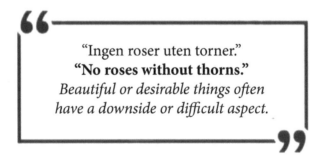

"Ingen roser uten torner."
"No roses without thorns."
*Beautiful or desirable things often
have a downside or difficult aspect.*

Word Search Puzzle: Travel & Transportation

AIRPORT
FLYPLASS
BUS
BUSS
TAXI
TAXI
TICKET
BILLETT
MAP
KART
CAR
BIL
METRO
T-BANE
BICYCLE
SYKKEL
DEPARTURE
AVGANG
ARRIVAL
ANKOMST
ROAD
VEI
PLATFORM
PLATTFORM
STATION
STASJON
TERMINAL
TERMINAL

```
O  K  I  S  H  T  B  L  A  N  I  M  R  E  T
X  T  X  A  Y  J  S  I  L  C  G  D  Y  B  Y
D  Q  A  I  J  K  O  M  L  L  F  A  H  F  X
U  U  T  R  R  O  K  D  O  L  K  O  L  I  D
I  N  A  P  Q  Z  U  E  M  K  E  R  C  I  V
L  G  L  O  S  U  B  P  L  Y  N  T  I  L  B
Q  A  F  R  F  G  R  A  S  H  K  A  T  F  R
S  J  N  T  L  J  P  R  L  A  V  I  R  R  A
F  M  A  I  P  L  A  T  F  O  R  M  C  R  L
E  Z  I  E  M  K  C  U  V  R  G  E  Z  A  S
A  E  N  T  T  R  E  R  M  Q  X  V  O  Q  B
V  A  A  H  F  K  E  E  S  O  D  T  O  Z  N
B  G  W  M  O  Y  Z  T  K  S  E  W  Y  W  S
Q  P  D  A  M  F  A  Z  V  T  R  N  K  E  A
N  D  L  P  F  S  V  F  O  A  F  H  M  W  C
M  D  A  A  J  Q  L  W  R  T  I  C  K  E  T
Q  H  Y  O  T  Y  E  G  T  I  I  M  U  S  T
Z  X  N  B  P  T  R  F  E  O  O  C  Q  K  O
Y  W  L  L  M  C  F  S  M  N  O  D  A  C  I
J  S  A  N  J  T  X  O  Z  Y  K  R  E  M  W
S  S  S  K  Y  O  V  X  R  K  T  C  H  R  Y
S  L  Y  U  H  T  R  X  K  M  W  F  A  W  U
C  T  D  W  B  I  J  F  L  J  K  D  O  Z  M
M  F  X  U  R  Y  V  N  K  J  Z  E  R  A  Y
A  T  W  C  F  M  A  Y  V  H  V  E  V  S  L
P  O  C  I  D  C  E  M  T  S  Y  G  K  N  I
L  L  X  U  Z  X  P  N  C  T  A  K  J  R  O
E  A  K  F  A  V  E  K  Z  N  D  I  W  R  Y
T  B  I  C  Y  C  L  E  G  H  C  V  S  I  B
Q  Y  R  B  J  E  N  R  A  C  Z  C  O  P  A
```

Correct Answers:

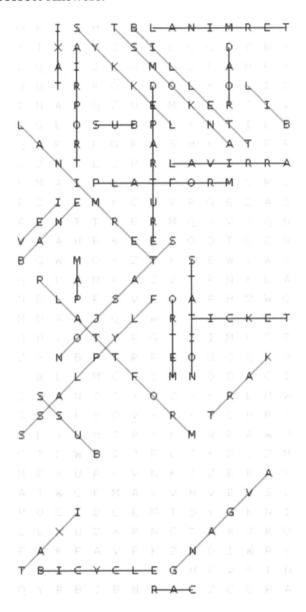

ACCOMMODATIONS

- CHECKING INTO A HOTEL -
- ASKING ABOUT ROOM AMENITIES -
- REPORTING ISSUES OR MAKING REQUESTS -

Hotel Check-In

233. I have a reservation under [Name].
Jeg har en reservasjon på navnet [Navn].
(Yai har en reh-ser-vah-shoon poh nahv-neh [Navn].)

234. Can I see some identification, please?
Kan jeg se litt identifikasjon, vær så snill?
(Kan yai seh litt ee-den-tee-fee-kah-shoon, vair soh snill?)

235. What time is check-in/check-out?
Når er innsjekking/utsjekking?
(Nor air in-shek-king/oot-shek-king?)

236. Is breakfast included in the room rate?
Er frokost inkludert i romprisen?
(Air fro-kost in-kloo-derth ee rom-pree-sen?)

237. Do you need a credit card for incidentals?
Trenger dere et kredittkort for tilleggsutgifter?
(Tren-ger deh-reh eht kreh-deet-kort for till-ehgs-oot-gif-ter?)

238. May I have a room key, please?
Kan jeg få en romnøkkel, vær så snill?
(Kan yai foh en rom-nuk-kel, vair soh snill?)

239. Could you call a bellhop for assistance?
Kan du tilkalle en piccolo for hjelp?
(Kan doo till-kal-leh en pee-koh-loh for yelp?)

240. Is there a shuttle service to the airport?
Er det en shuttle-service til flyplassen?
(*Air deht en shut-le ser-vee-seh teel flee-plahs-sen?*)

> **Fun Fact:** Norway has won more Winter Olympic medals than any other country.

Room Amenities

241. Can I request a non-smoking room?
Kan jeg be om et røykfritt rom?
(*Kan yai beh ohm eht røyk-freet room?*)

242. Is there a mini-fridge in the room?
Er det et minibar i rommet?
(*Air deht eht mee-nee-bar ee rom-meh?*)

243. Do you provide free Wi-Fi access?
Tilbyr dere gratis Wi-Fi-tilgang?
(*Till-beer deh-reh grah-tis Wee-Fee teel-gong?*)

244. Can I have an extra pillow or blanket?
Kan jeg få en ekstra pute eller teppe?
(*Kan yai foh en ehk-strah poo-teh eh-ler teh-peh?*)

245. Is there a hairdryer in the bathroom?
Er det en hårføner på badet?
(*Air deht en hor-fø-ner poh bah-deht?*)

246. What's the TV channel lineup?
Hva er TV-kanaloversikten?
(*Vah air Tee-Vee kah-nahl-oh-ver-sik-ten?*)

247. Are toiletries like shampoo provided?
Er toalettartikler som sjampo inkludert?
(*Air toh-ah-leh-tahr-tee-kler sohm shahm-poh in-kloo-derth?*)

248. Is room service available 24/7?
Er romservice tilgjengelig hele døgnet?
(*Air rom-ser-vee-seh teel-yeng-eh-lee heh-leh dug-neht?*)

> **Fun Fact:** Norwegian folklore is rich with tales of trolls, mythical creatures said to inhabit the forests and mountains.

Reporting Issues

249. There's a problem with the air conditioning.
Det er et problem med klimaanlegget.
(*Deht air eht proh-blem meh klee-mah-an-leh-geht.*)

250. The shower is not working properly.
Dusjen fungerer ikke ordentlig.
(*Doosh-yen foon-geh-rer eek-keh or-den-tlee.*)

251. My room key card isn't functioning.
Romnøkkelkortet mitt fungerer ikke.
(*Rom-nøk-kel-kor-teh meet foon-geh-rer eek-keh.*)

252.   There's a leak in the bathroom.
Det er en lekkasje på badet.
(*Deht air en lehk-kah-sheh poh bah-deht.*)

253.   The TV remote is not responding.
Fjernkontrollen til TV-en reagerer ikke.
(*Fyern-kohn-trohl-len teel Tee-Vee-en rah-ah-gehr-er eek-keh.*)

254.   Can you fix the broken light in my room?
Kan dere reparere den ødelagte lampen i rommet mitt?
(*Kan deh-reh reh-pah-reh-reh dehn ø-deh-lahg-teh lahm-pen ee rom-met meet?*)

255.   I need assistance with my luggage.
Jeg trenger hjelp med bagasjen min.
(*Yai tren-ger yelp meh bah-gah-syen meen.*)

256.   There's a strange noise coming from next door.
Det kommer en merkelig lyd fra rommet ved siden av.
(*Deht kohm-mer en meh-reh-lee lyd frah rom-met vehd see-den ahv.*)

Making Requests

257.   Can I have a wake-up call at 7 AM?
Kan jeg få en vekkeklokke klokken syv om morgenen?
(*Kan yai foh en vehk-keh-kloh-kkeh kloh-ken seev ohm mohr-geh-nen?*)

> **Fun Fact:** Norwegians are among the top consumers of coffee in the world.

258. Please send extra towels to my room.
Kan dere sende ekstra håndklær til rommet mitt.
(Kan deh-reh sen-deh ehk-strah hohn-klær teel rom-met meet.)

259. Could you arrange a taxi for tomorrow?
Kan dere bestille en taxi for meg til i morgen?
(Kan deh-reh behs-teel-leh en tak-see for may teel ee mohr-gen?)

260. I'd like to extend my stay for two more nights.
Jeg ønsker å forlenge oppholdet mitt med to netter til.
(Yai urn-sker oh for-len-geh opp-hol-det meet meh toh net-ter teel.)

> **Idiomatic Expression:** "Å gå rundt grøten." -
> Meaning: "To beat around the bush."
> (Literal translation: "To walk around the porridge.")

261. Is it possible to change my room?
Er det mulig å bytte rommet mitt?
(Air deht moo-leeg oh bee-tee rom-met meet?)

262. Can I have a late check-out at 2 PM?
Kan jeg få en sen utsjekking klokken to på ettermiddagen?
(Kan yai foh en sen oot-shek-king kloh-ken toh poh eh-ter-mee-dah-gen?)

263. I need an iron and ironing board.
Jeg trenger et strykejern og et strykebrett.
(Yai tren-ger eht stryk-eh-yarn oh eht stryk-eh-brett.)

264. Could you provide directions to [location]?
Kan dere gi meg veibeskrivelse til [sted]?
(Kan deh-reh gee may vye-beh-skree-vehl-seh teel [stehd]?)

Room Types and Preferences

265.   I'd like to book a single room, please.
        Jeg ønsker å bestille et enkeltrom, vær så snill.
        (Yai urn-sker oh beh-stee-leh eht en-kel-trom, vair soh snill.)

266.   Do you have any suites available?
        Har dere noen suiter tilgjengelige?
        (Har deh-reh noo-en swee-ter teel-yeng-eh-lee-geh?)

267.   Is there a room with a view of the city?
        Finnes det et rom med utsikt over byen?
        (Fee-nes deht eht rom meh oot-seekt oh-ver bee-yen?)

268.   Is breakfast included in the room rate?
        Er frokost inkludert i romprisen?
        (Air fro-kost in-kloo-derth ee rom-pree-sen?)

269.   Can I request a room on a higher floor?
        Kan jeg be om et rom i en høyere etasje?
        (Kan yai beh ohm eht rom ee en hoy-eh-reh eh-tah-sheh?)

270.   Is there an option for a smoking room?
        Finnes det et røykerom tilgjengelig?
        (Fee-nes deht eht roy-keh-rom teel-yeng-eh-lee-geh?)

> **Travel Story:** During a cozy night in a Tromsø pub,
> locals shared tales of the Northern Lights, or "Nordlyset,"
> a magical experience in the Arctic Circle.

271.   Are there connecting rooms for families?
Har dere sammenhengende rom for familier?
(Har deh-reh sahm-men-heng-en-deh rom for fah-mee-lee-er?)

272.   I'd prefer a king-size bed.
Jeg foretrekker en king-size seng.
(Yai for-eh-trek-ker en keeng-size seng.)

273.   Is there a bathtub in any of the rooms?
Er det et badekar i noen av rommene?
(Air deht eht bah-deh-kar ee noo-en ahv rom-meh-neh?)

Hotel Facilities and Services

274.   What time does the hotel restaurant close?
Når stenger hotellets restaurant?
(Nor sten-ger ho-tehl-lets res-tau-rant?)

275.   Is there a fitness center in the hotel?
Er det et treningssenter i hotellet?
(Air deht eht treh-neengs-sen-ter ee ho-tehl-let?)

276.   Can I access the pool as a guest?
Kan jeg bruke svømmebassenget som gjest?
(Kan yai broo-keh svøm-meh-bah-sen-geht sohm yest?)

277.   Do you offer laundry facilities?
Tilbyr dere vaskeritjenester?
(Till-beer deh-reh vahs-keh-ree-tyen-ehs-ter?)

278. Is parking available on-site?
Er det parkering tilgjengelig på stedet?
(*Air deht pahr-keh-ring teel-yeng-eh-lee poh steh-det?*)

279. Is room cleaning provided daily?
Blir rommet rengjort daglig?
(*Bleer rom-met reng-yort dahg-lee?*)

280. Can I use the business center?
Kan jeg bruke forretningssenteret?
(*Kan yai broo-keh for-reht-neengs-sen-teh-ret?*)

281. Are pets allowed in the hotel?
Er kjæledyr tillatt i hotellet?
(*Air yæ-leh-deer till-aht ee ho-tehl-let?*)

> **Travel Story:** At a quaint café in Trondheim, a server described their famous cinnamon buns as "Søt som synden," meaning "Sweet as sin."

Payment and Check-Out

282. Can I have the bill, please?
Kan jeg få regningen, vær så snill?
(*Kan yai foh reh-geen-gen, vair soh snill?*)

283. Do you accept credit cards?
Tar dere kredittkort?
(*Tahr deh-reh kreh-deet-kort?*)

284. Can I pay in cash?
Kan jeg betale kontant?
(Kan yai beh-tah-leh kohn-tahnt?)

285. Is there a security deposit required?
Er det nødvendig med et sikkerhetsdepositum?
(Air deht nød-ven-dee meh eht sik-ker-hets-deh-poh-see-toom?)

286. Can I get a receipt for my stay?
Kan jeg få en kvittering for oppholdet mitt?
(Kan yai foh en kvit-teh-ring for opp-hol-det meet?)

287. What's the check-out time?
Når er utsjekkingstidspunktet?
(Nor air oot-shek-kings-teeds-poonk-teh?)

288. Is late check-out an option?
Er det mulig med sen utsjekking?
(Air deht moo-leeg meh sen oot-shek-king?)

289. Can I settle my bill in advance?
Kan jeg betale regningen min på forhånd?
(Kan yai beh-tah-leh reh-geen-gen meen poh for-hohnd?)

Booking Accommodations

290. I'd like to make a reservation.
Jeg ønsker å gjøre en reservasjon.
(Yai urn-sker oh yu-reh en reh-ser-vah-shoon.)

291.	How much is the room rate per night?
Hva er romprisen per natt?
(*Vah air rom-pree-sen pair naht?*)

292.	Can I book online or by phone?
Kan jeg bestille på nett eller telefon?
(*Kan yai beh-stee-leh poh net eh-ler teh-leh-fohn?*)

293.	Are there any special promotions?
Har dere noen spesielle tilbud?
(*Har deh-reh noo-en speh-see-eh-leh teel-bood?*)

294.	Is breakfast included in the booking?
Er frokost inkludert i bookingen?
(*Air fro-kost in-kloo-derth ee boo-keen-gen?*)

295.	Can you confirm my reservation?
Kan dere bekrefte reservasjonen min?
(*Kan deh-reh beh-kref-teh reh-ser-vah-shoh-nen meen?*)

296.	What's the cancellation policy?
Hva er avbestillingspolitikken?
(*Vah air ahv-beh-stee-leengs-poh-lee-teek-ken?*)

297.	I'd like to modify my booking.
Jeg vil gjerne endre bookingen min.
(*Yai vil yarn-eh en-dreh boo-keen-gen meen?*)

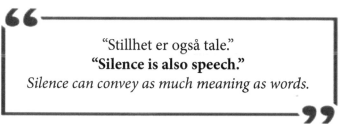

"Stillhet er også tale."
"Silence is also speech."
Silence can convey as much meaning as words.

Mini Lesson:
Basic Grammar Principles in Norwegian #1

Introduction:

Norwegian, a North Germanic language spoken primarily in Norway, offers a blend of simplicity and complexity in its linguistic structure. It is essential for anyone looking to connect with Norwegian culture and society. This lesson provides an introduction to the fundamental grammar principles of Norwegian, setting the stage for beginners to start their journey into this captivating language.

1. Nouns and Gender:

Norwegian nouns are divided into three genders: masculine, feminine, and neuter. The articles "en" (masculine), "ei" (feminine), and "et" (neuter) are used for indefinite singular forms:

- *En hund (a dog) - masculine*
- *Ei bok (a book) - feminine*
- *Et hus (a house) - neuter*

2. Definite Articles:

The definite article in Norwegian is typically a suffix attached to the noun:

- *Hunden (the dog)*
- *Boka or boken (the book)*
- *Huset (the house)*

3. Personal Pronouns:

Norwegian personal pronouns change according to their function in a sentence:

- *Jeg (I)*
- *Du (you - singular)*
- *Han/Hun/Den/Det (he/she/it, with 'den' for common gender and 'det' for neuter)*
- *Vi (we)*
- *Dere (you - plural)*
- *De (they)*

4. Verb Conjugation:

Norwegian verbs generally do not conjugate according to person or number. However, they change form according to tense:

- *Jeg er (I am)*
- *Du er (You are)*
- *Han/Hun/Den/Det er (He/She/It is)*
- *Vi er (We are)*
- *Dere er (You all are)*
- *De er (They are)*

5. Tenses:

Norwegian verbs express various tenses, including present, past, and future:

- *Jeg leser (I read)*
- *Jeg leste (I read/I was reading - past)*
- *Jeg vil lese (I will read)*

6. Negation:

To negate a statement in Norwegian, the word "ikke" (not) is placed after the verb:

- *Jeg forstår ikke (I don't understand)*
- *De snakker ikke norsk (They don't speak Norwegian)*

7. Questions:

Norwegian questions are formed by inverting the subject and verb or using question words:

- *Snakker du norsk? (Do you speak Norwegian?)*
- *Hvor er badet? (Where is the bathroom?)*

8. Plurals:

Plural forms in Norwegian can be formed by adding -er, -e, or sometimes with no change:

- *En bil (a car) -> Biler (cars)*
- *Et bord (a table) -> Bord (tables)*

Conclusion:

Grasping these basic aspects of Norwegian grammar is a critical step in your language learning journey. Regular practice, along with exposure to Norwegian media and conversations, will further enhance your understanding and proficiency. Lykke til! (Good luck!)

SHOPPING

- BARGAINING AND HAGGLING -
- DESCRIBING ITEMS AND SIZES -
- MAKING PURCHASES AND PAYMENTS -

Bargaining

298. Can you give me a discount?
Kan dere gi meg en rabatt?
(Kan deh-reh gee may en rah-baht?)

299. What's your best price?
Hva er deres beste pris?
(Vah air deh-res behs-teh preece?)

300. Is this the final price?
Er dette den endelige prisen?
(Air deh-teh dehn en-deh-lee-geh pree-sen?)

> **Idiomatic Expression:** "Å stå med skjegget i postkassen."
> - Meaning: "To be caught in a difficult situation."
> (Literal translation: "To stand with one's beard in the mailbox.")

301. I'd like to negotiate the price.
Jeg ønsker å forhandle om prisen.
(Yai urn-sker oh for-hahn-leh ohm pree-sen.)

302. Can you do any better on the price?
Kan dere komme med en bedre pris?
(Kan deh-reh kohm-meh meh en beh-dreh preece?)

303. Are there any promotions or deals?
Har dere noen kampanjer eller tilbud?
(Har deh-reh noo-en kahm-pahn-yehr eh-ler teel-bood?)

304. What's the lowest you can go?
Hva er det laveste dere kan gå?
(Vah air deht lah-ves-teh deh-reh kan goh?)

305. I'm on a budget. Can you lower the price?
Jeg har et begrenset budsjett. Kan dere senke prisen?
(*Yai har eht beh-gren-set boo-syet. Kan deh-reh sen-keh pree-sen?*)

306. Do you offer any discounts for cash payments?
Tilbyr dere rabatt for kontantbetaling?
(*Till-beer deh-reh rah-baht for kohn-tahnt-beh-tah-leeng?*)

307. Can you match the price from your competitor?
Kan dere matche prisen til deres konkurrent?
(*Kan deh-reh mah-cheh pree-sen teel deh-res kohn-koo-rent?*)

Item Descriptions

308. Can you tell me about this product?
Kan dere fortelle meg om dette produktet?
(*Kan deh-reh for-tehl-leh may ohm deh-teh pro-dook-teh?*)

309. What are the specifications of this item?
Hva er spesifikasjonene til denne varen?
(*Vah air speh-see-fee-kah-syo-neh-neh teel dehn-neh vah-ren?*)

310. Is this available in different colors?
Er dette tilgjengelig i forskjellige farger?
(*Air deh-teh teel-yeng-eh-lee ee for-shjel-lee-geh fahr-ger?*)

311. Can you explain how this works?
Kan dere forklare hvordan dette fungerer?
(*Kan deh-reh for-klah-reh vohr-dan deh-teh foon-gehr-er?*)

312. What's the material of this item?
Hva er dette produktet laget av?
(Vah air deh-teh pro-dook-teh lah-get ahv?)

313. Are there any warranties or guarantees?
Er det noen garantier eller forsikringer for dette produktet?
(Air deht noo-en gah-ran-tee-er eh-ler for-see-kehr-een-ger for deh-teh pro-dook-teh?)

314. Does it come with accessories?
Følger det med tilbehør?
(Fuhl-ger deht meh teel-beh-hør?)

315. Can you show me how to use this?
Kan du vise meg hvordan dette brukes?
(Kan doo vee-seh may vohr-dan deh-teh broo-kes?)

316. Are there any size options available?
Finnes det forskjellige størrelser tilgjengelig?
(Fee-nes deht for-sjel-lee-geh stur-rel-ser teel-yeng-eh-lee-geh?)

317. Can you describe the features of this product?
Kan du beskrive funksjonene til dette produktet?
(Kan doo beh-skree-veh foonk-shoh-neh-neh teel deh-teh pro-dook-teh?)

Payments

318. I'd like to pay with a credit card.
Jeg vil gjerne betale med kredittkort.
(Yai vil yarn-eh beh-tah-leh meh kreh-deet-kort.)

319.   Do you accept debit cards?
Tar dere debetkort?
(*Tahr deh-reh deh-beht-kort?*)

320.   Can I pay in cash?
Kan jeg betale kontant?
(*Kan yai beh-tah-leh kohn-tahnt?*)

> **Idiomatic Expression:** "Å snakke rett fra leveren." -
> Meaning: "To speak frankly."
> (Literal translation: "To speak straight from the liver.")

321.   What's your preferred payment method?
Hva foretrekker dere som betalingsmåte?
(*Vah for-eh-trek-ker deh-reh sohm beh-tah-leengs-moh-teh?*)

322.   Is there an extra charge for using a card?
Er det ekstra kostnad for å bruke kort?
(*Air deht ehk-strah koh-stahd for oh broo-keh kort?*)

323.   Can I split the payment into installments?
Kan jeg dele opp betalingen i avdrag?
(*Kan yai deh-leh opp beh-tah-leen-gen ee ahv-drahg?*)

324.   Do you offer online payment options?
Tilbyr dere online betalingsalternativer?
(*Till-beer deh-reh on-line beh-tah-leengs-al-ter-nah-tee-vehr?*)

325.   Can I get a receipt for this purchase?
Kan jeg få en kvittering for dette kjøpet?
(*Kan yai foh en kvit-teh-ring for deh-teh kye-peh?*)

326.   Are there any additional fees?
       Er det noen ekstra avgifter?
       (*Air deht noo-en ehk-strah ahv-gee-fter?*)

327.   Is there a minimum purchase amount for card payments?
       Er det et minimumskjøp for betaling med kort?
       (*Air deht eht mee-nee-mooms-kjøp for beh-tah-leeng meh kort?*)

>   **Travel Story:** In the historic streets of Stavanger, a guide
>   shared tales of Viking explorers with "De gamle
>   sjøfarerne," meaning "The old seafarers."

Asking for Recommendations

328.   Can you recommend something popular?
       Kan du anbefale noe populært?
       (*Kan doo ahn-beh-fah-leh noo-eh poh-poo-lær?*)

329.   What's your best-selling product?
       Hva er deres bestselgende produkt?
       (*Vah air deh-res behst-sel-gen-deh pro-dookt?*)

330.   Do you have any customer favorites?
       Har dere noen kundefavoritter?
       (*Har deh-reh noo-en koon-deh-fah-vo-rit-ter?*)

331.   Is there a brand you would suggest?
       Vil du anbefale et spesielt merke?
       (*Vill doo ahn-beh-fah-leh eht speh-see-ehlt mer-keh?*)

332. Could you point me to high-quality items?
Kan du vise meg til høykvalitetsprodukter?
(Kan doo vee-seh may teel hoy-kvah-lee-tehts-pro-dook-ter?)

333. What do most people choose in this category?
Hva velger de fleste i denne kategorien?
(Vah vel-ger deh fles-teh ee dehn-neh kah-toh-ree-ehn?)

334. Are there any special recommendations?
Har dere noen spesielle anbefalinger?
(Har deh-reh noo-en speh-see-eh-leh ahn-beh-fah-leen-ger?)

335. Can you tell me what's trendy right now?
Kan du fortelle meg hva som er trendy akkurat nå?
(Kan doo for-tell-eh may vah sohm air tren-dee ah-koo-raht noh?)

336. What's your personal favorite here?
Hva er din personlige favoritt her?
(Vah air deen pehr-soh-nee-lee-geh fah-voh-ritt hair?)

337. Any suggestions for a gift?
Har du noen forslag til en gave?
(Har doo noo-en for-shlahg teel en gah-veh?)

Language Learning Tip: Celebrate Small Wins - Every new word or correctly constructed sentence is progress.

Returns and Exchanges

338. I'd like to return this item.
Jeg vil gjerne returnere dette produktet.
(*Yai vil yarn-eh reh-too-neh-reh deh-teh pro-dook-teh.*)

339. Can I exchange this for a different size?
Kan jeg bytte dette mot en annen størrelse?
(*Kan yai bee-tee deh-teh moht en ahn-nen stur-rel-seh?*)

340. What's your return policy?
Hva er deres returpolicy?
(*Vah air deh-res reh-tour-po-lee-see?*)

341. Is there a time limit for returns?
Er det en tidsfrist for returer?
(*Air deht en teeds-freest for reh-too-ehr?*)

342. Do I need a receipt for a return?
Trenger jeg en kvittering for å returnere?
(*Tren-ger yai en kvit-teh-ring for oh reh-too-neh-reh?*)

343. Is there a restocking fee for returns?
Er det et gebyr for å fylle på lageret ved returer?
(*Air deht eht yeh-byer for oh fih-leh poh lah-gehr-et ved reh-too-ehr?*)

344. Can I get a refund or store credit?
Kan jeg få tilbakebetaling eller butikkredit?
(*Kan yai foh til-bah-keh-beh-tah-leeng eh-ler boo-teek-kreh-deet?*)

345. Do you offer exchanges without receipts?
      Tilbyr dere bytte uten kvittering?
      (*Till-beer deh-reh bee-tee oo-ten kvit-teh-ring?*)

346. What's the process for returning a defective item?
      Hva er prosessen for å returnere en defekt vare?
      (*Vah air proh-sess-en for oh reh-too-neh-reh en deh-fekt vah-reh?*)

347. Can I return an online purchase in-store?
      Kan jeg returnere et onlinekjøp i butikken?
      (*Kan yai reh-too-neh-reh eht on-line-kjøp ee boo-teek-ken?*)

> **Travel Story:** At a traditional bakery in Trondheim, the
> baker praised his goods with "Bakt med tradisjon,"
> meaning "Baked with tradition."

Shopping for Souvenirs

348. I'm looking for local souvenirs.
      Jeg ser etter lokale suvenirer.
      (*Yai seer eh-ter loh-kah-leh soo-veh-neer-er.*)

349. What's a popular souvenir from this place?
      Hva er en populær suvenir fra dette stedet?
      (*Vah air en poh-poo-lær soo-veh-neer frah deh-teh steh-det?*)

350. Do you have any handmade souvenirs?
      Har dere håndlagde suvenirer?
      (*Har deh-reh hond-lahg-deh soo-veh-neer-er?*)

351. Are there any traditional items here?
Har dere tradisjonelle gjenstander her?
(Har deh-reh trah-dee-syo-nell-eh yen-stahn-der hair?)

352. Can you suggest a unique souvenir?
Kan du foreslå en unik suvenir?
(Kan doo foh-reh-sloh en oo-neek soo-veh-neer?)

353. I want something that represents this city.
Jeg ønsker noe som representerer denne byen.
(Yai urn-sker noo-eh sohm reh-preh-sen-teh-rer dehn-neh bee-yen.)

354. Are there souvenirs for a specific landmark?
Har dere suvenirer for et spesifikt landemerke?
(Har deh-reh soo-veh-neer-er for eht speh-see-feekt lahnd-eh-mer-keh?)

355. Can you show me souvenirs with cultural significance?
Kan du vise meg suvenirer med kulturell betydning?
(Kan doo vee-seh may soo-veh-neer-er meh kool-too-rell beh-teed-neeng?)

356. Do you offer personalized souvenirs?
Tilbyr dere personlige suvenirer?
(Till-beer deh-reh pehr-soh-nee-lee-geh soo-veh-neer-er?)

357. What's the price range for souvenirs?
Hva er prisklassen for suvenirer?
(Vah air preece-klahs-sen for soo-veh-neer-er?)

Cultural Insight: Norway has a rich literary and artistic heritage, with authors like Henrik Ibsen and painters like Edvard Munch.

Shopping Online

358. How do I place an order online?
Hvordan bestiller jeg online?
(*Vor-dan beh-stee-ler yai on-line?*)

359. What's the website for online shopping?
Hva er nettsiden for netthandel?
(*Vah air net-see-den for nett-hahn-del?*)

360. Do you offer free shipping?
Tilbyr dere gratis frakt?
(*Till-beer deh-reh grah-teess frahkt?*)

361. Are there any online discounts or promotions?
Er det noen nettrabatter eller kampanjer?
(*Air deht noo-en nett-rah-bat-ter eh-ler kahm-pahn-yehr?*)

362. Can I track my online order?
Kan jeg spore min onlinebestilling?
(*Kan yai spoh-reh meen on-line-beh-stee-leeng?*)

363. What's the return policy for online purchases?
Hva er returpolitikken for nettkjøp?
(*Vah air reh-toor-poh-lee-teek-ken for nett-kjøp?*)

364. Do you accept various payment methods online?
Aksepterer dere ulike betalingsmetoder online?
(*Ahk-sep-teh-rer deh-reh oo-lee-keh beh-tah-leengs-meh-toh-der on-line?*)

365. Is there a customer support hotline for online orders?
Finnes det en kundestøttelinje for nettkjøp?
(*Fee-nes deht en koon-deh-støtte-lee-neh for nett-kjøp?*)

> **Idiomatic Expression:** "Å få kald føtter." -
> Meaning: "To get cold feet."
> (Literal translation: "To get cold feet.")

366. Can I change or cancel my online order?
Kan jeg endre eller kansellere min onlinebestilling?
(*Kan yai en-dreh eh-ler kan-seh-leh-reh meen
on-line-beh-stee-leeng?*)

367. What's the delivery time for online purchases?
Hva er leveringstiden for nettkjøp?
(*Vah air leh-veh-rings-tee-den for nett-kjøp?*)

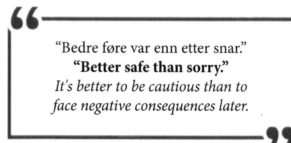

"Bedre føre var enn etter snar."
"Better safe than sorry."
*It's better to be cautious than to
face negative consequences later.*

Cross Word Puzzle: Shopping

(Provide the Norwegian translation for the following English words)

Down

2. - BOUTIQUE
4. - PRICE
5. - CART
9. - CUSTOMER
10. - CASHIER
12. - SALE
13. - CLOTHING

Across

1. - WALLET
3. - PURCHASE
6. - STORE
7. - DISCOUNT
8. - COUNTER
11. - BRAND
12. - SHOPPER
13. - RECEIPT

Correct Answers:

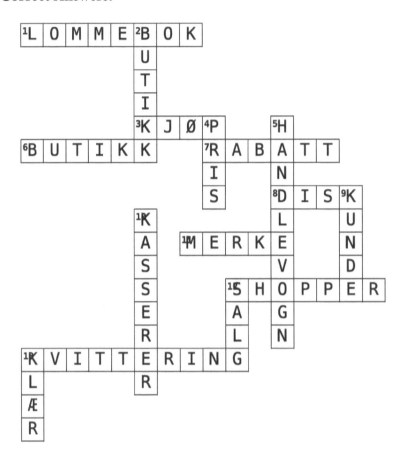

EMERGENCIES

- SEEKING HELP IN CASE OF AN EMERGENCY -
- REPORTING ACCIDENTS OR HEALTH ISSUES -
- CONTACTING AUTHORITIES OR MEDICAL SERVICES -

Getting Help in Emergencies

368.   Call an ambulance, please.
Ring en ambulanse, vær så snill.
(Reeng en ahm-boo-lahn-seh, vair soh snill.)

> **Language Learning Tip:** Write in Norwegian - Start a journal where you write daily in Norwegian.

369.   I need a doctor right away.
Jeg trenger en lege med en gang.
(Yai tren-ger en leh-geh meh en gahng.)

370.   Is there a hospital nearby?
Er det et sykehus i nærheten?
(Air deht et see-keh-hoos ee nær-het-en?)

371.   Help! I've lost my way.
Hjelp! Jeg har gått meg vill.
(Yelp! Yai har gott may veell.)

372.   Can you call the police?
Kan du ringe politiet?
(Kan doo reeng-eh poh-lee-teet?)

373.   Someone, please call for help.
Noen, vær så snill, ring etter hjelp.
(No-en, vair soh snill, reeng eh-ter yelp.)

374.   My friend is hurt, we need assistance.
Vennen min er skadet, vi trenger hjelp.
(Ven-nen meen air shah-det, vee tren-ger yelp.)

375. I've been robbed; I need the authorities.
Jeg har blitt ranet; jeg trenger myndighetene.
(*Yai har bleett rah-net; yai tren-ger moon-dee-heh-teh-neh.*)

376. Please, I need immediate assistance.
Vær så snill, jeg trenger umiddelbar hjelp.
(*Vair soh snill, yai tren-ger oo-meed-del-bar yelp.*)

377. Is there a fire station nearby?
Er det en brannstasjon i nærheten?
(*Air deht en bran-stah-shoon ee nær-het-en?*)

Reporting Incidents

378. I've witnessed an accident.
Jeg har vært vitne til en ulykke.
(*Yai har vært vit-neh teel en ool-ik-keh.*)

379. There's been a car crash.
Det har vært en bilulykke.
(*Deht har vært en beel-ool-ik-keh.*)

380. We need to report a fire.
Vi må melde fra om en brann.
(*Vee moh mel-deh frah ohm en bran.*)

381. Someone has stolen my wallet.
Noen har stjålet lommeboken min.
(*No-en har shoh-let lomm-eh-boh-ken meen.*)

382.   I need to report a lost passport.
Jeg må rapportere et mistet pass.
(Yai moh rah-pohr-teh-reh eht mees-teht pahss.)

383.   There's a suspicious person here.
Det er en mistenkelig person her.
(Deht air en mees-ten-eh-lee person hair.)

384.   I've found a lost child.
Jeg har funnet et bortkommet barn.
(Yai har foon-net eht bort-kom-met barn.)

385.   Can you help me report a missing person?
Kan du hjelpe meg med å rapportere en savnet person?
(Kan doo yel-peh may meh oh rah-pohr-teh-reh en sah-vnet person?)

386.   We've had a break-in at our home.
Vi har hatt et innbrudd i vårt hjem.
(Vee har haht eht in-brood ee voort yehm.)

387.   I need to report a damaged vehicle.
Jeg må rapportere et skadet kjøretøy.
(Yai moh rah-pohr-teh-reh eht shah-det yø-reh-tøy.)

Contacting Authorities

388.   I'd like to speak to the police.
Jeg vil snakke med politiet.
(Yai veel snahk-keh meh poh-lee-teet.)

389. I need to contact the embassy.
Jeg må kontakte ambassaden.
(*Yai moh kohn-tahk-teh ahm-bahs-sah-den.*)

390. Can you connect me to the fire department?
Kan du koble meg til brannvesenet?
(*Kan doo koh-bleh may teel brahn-veh-seh-net?*)

391. We need to reach animal control.
Vi må kontakte dyrekontrollen.
(*Vee moh kohn-tahk-teh dee-reh-kohn-troh-len.*)

392. How do I get in touch with the coast guard?
Hvordan tar jeg kontakt med kystvakten?
(*Vor-dan tar yai kohn-tahkt meh kyst-vahk-ten?*)

393. I'd like to report a noise complaint.
Jeg vil melde fra om en støyklage.
(*Yai veel mehl-deh frah ohm en støy-klaa-geh.*)

394. I need to contact child protective services.
Jeg må kontakte barnevernet.
(*Yai moh kohn-tahk-teh bar-neh-ver-net.*)

395. Is there a hotline for disaster relief?
Finnes det en nødtelefon for katastrofehjelp?
(*Fee-nes deht en nød-teh-leh-foon for kah-tah-stroh-feh-yelp?*)

> **Fun Fact:** Norway is one of the world's largest exporters of seafood, especially salmon.

396. I want to report a hazardous situation.
Jeg vil rapportere en farlig situasjon.
(*Yai veel rah-pohr-teh-reh en fah-ree-leeg see-too-ah-shoon.*)

397. I need to reach the environmental agency.
Jeg må kontakte miljøetaten.
(*Yai moh kohn-tahk-teh meel-yø-eh-tah-ten.*)

> **Travel Story:** At a rustic cabin in Hardangervidda, a local storyteller enchanted guests with "Gamle fjellmyter," meaning "Old mountain myths."

Medical Emergencies

398. I'm feeling very ill.
Jeg føler meg veldig syk.
(*Yai fø-lehr may vehl-dee seek.*)

399. There's been an accident; we need a medic.
Det har vært en ulykke; vi trenger en lege.
(*Deht har vært en ool-ik-keh; vee tren-ger en leh-geh.*)

400. Call 112; it's a medical emergency.
Ring 112; det er en medisinsk nødsituasjon.
(*Reeng ett-hunn-oh-to; deht air en meh-dee-seensk nød-see-too-ah-shoon.*)

> **Fun Fact:** The paperclip was invented by Norwegian Johann Vaaler.

401. We need an ambulance right away.
Vi trenger en ambulanse med en gang.
(*Vee tren-ger en ahm-boo-lahn-seh meh en gahng.*)

402. I'm having trouble breathing.
Jeg har problemer med å puste.
(*Yai har proh-bleh-mer meh oh poos-teh.*)

403. Someone has lost consciousness.
Noen har mistet bevisstheten.
(*No-en har mees-teht beh-vees-steh-ten.*)

404. I think it's a heart attack; call for help.
Jeg tror det er et hjerteinfarkt; ring etter hjelp.
(*Yai tror deht air eht yehr-teh-een-fahrkt; reeng eh-ter yelp.*)

405. There's been a severe injury.
Det har vært en alvorlig skade.
(*Deht har vært en ahl-vor-lee skah-deh.*)

406. I need immediate medical attention.
Jeg trenger øyeblikkelig medisinsk hjelp.
(*Yai tren-ger øye-blikk-leeg meh-dee-seensk yelp.*)

407. Is there a first-aid station nearby?
Finnes det en førstehjelpsstasjon i nærheten?
(*Fee-nes deht en førs-teh-hyelps-stah-shoon ee nær-het-en?*)

> **Idiomatic Expression:** "Å skyte fra hoften." -
> Meaning: "To speak or act without thinking."
> (Literal translation: "To shoot from the hip.")

Fire and Safety

408.　There's a fire; call 112!
Det er brann; ring 112!
(Deht air brahn; reeng ett-hunn-oh-to!)

409.　We need to evacuate the building.
Vi må evakuere bygningen.
(Vee moh eh-vah-koo-eh-reh bueg-neeng-en.)

410.　Fire extinguisher, quick!
Brannslukker, fort!
(Brahn-sloohk-ker, forht!)

411.　I smell gas; we need to leave.
Jeg lukter gass; vi må gå.
(Yai look-ter gahss; vee moh goh.)

> **Fun Fact:** The Norwegian language has some unique words, like "utepils" - drinking a beer outside.

412.　Can you contact the fire department?
Kan du kontakte brannvesenet?
(Kan doo kohn-tahk-teh brahn-veh-seh-net?)

413.　There's a hazardous spill; we need help.
Det er et farlig utslipp; vi trenger hjelp.
(Deht air eht fah-ree-leeg oot-sleep; vee tren-ger yelp.)

414.　Is there a fire escape route?
Finnes det en nødutgangsrute?
(Fee-nes deht en nød-oot-gahngs-roo-teh?)

415. This area is not safe; we need to move.
Dette området er ikke trygt; vi må flytte oss.
(*Deh-teh ohm-roh-deh air eek-keh trygt; vee moh flee-teh oss.*)

416. Alert, there's a potential explosion.
Varsel, det er risiko for en eksplosjon.
(*Vahr-sel, deht air ree-see-koh forh en eks-ploh-shohn.*)

417. I see smoke; we need assistance.
Jeg ser røyk; vi trenger hjelp.
(*Yai sear røyk; vee tren-ger yelp.*)

Natural Disasters

418. It's an earthquake; take cover!
Det er jordskjelv; søk dekning!
(*Deht air yords-shehlv; søk dehk-ning!*)

419. We're experiencing a tornado; find shelter.
Det kommer en tornado; finn ly.
(*Deht kohm-mer en tor-nah-doh; feen lee.*)

420. Flood warning; move to higher ground.
Flomvarsel; flytt til høyere grunn.
(*Flohmm-var-sel; flee-tt teel hoy-eh-reh groon.*)

421. We need to prepare for a hurricane.
Vi må forberede oss på en orkan.
(*Vee moh for-beh-reh-deh oss poh en or-kahn.*)

422. This is a tsunami alert; head inland.
Dette er en tsunami-varsel; dra innover i landet.
(*Deh-teh air en tsoo-nah-mee vahr-sel; drah in-noh-ver ee lah-net.*)

> **Fun Fact:** Norway is famous for its medieval wooden stave churches.

423. It's a wildfire; evacuate immediately.
Det er en skogbrann; evakuer umiddelbart.
(*Deht air en skohg-brahn; eh-vah-kew-er oo-mee-del-bahrt.*)

424. There's a volcanic eruption; take precautions.
Det er et vulkanutbrudd; ta forholdsregler.
(*Deht air eht vool-kahn-oout-broodd; tah for-holds-rehg-lehr.*)

425. We've had an avalanche; help needed.
Det har vært et snøskred; vi trenger hjelp.
(*Deht hahr vært eht snø-shrehd; vee tren-ger yelp.*)

426. Earthquake aftershock; stay indoors.
Etterskjelv etter jordskjelv; hold deg innendørs.
(*Eh-ter-shehlv eh-ter yord-shehlv; hohld deh in-en-dørs.*)

427. Severe thunderstorm; seek shelter.
Kraftig tordenvær; søk ly.
(*Krahf-teeg tohr-den-vær; søk lee.*)

> **Idiomatic Expression:** "Å se rødt." -
> Meaning: "To become very angry."
> (Literal translation: "To see red.")

Emergency Services Information

428. What's the emergency hotline number?
Hva er nummeret til nødtelefonen?
(Vah air noo-meh-ret teel nød-teh-leh-foh-nen?)

429. Where's the nearest police station?
Hvor er den nærmeste politistasjonen?
(Vor air dehn nær-mes-teh poh-lee-tees-tah-shoh-nen?)

430. How do I contact the fire department?
Hvordan kontakter jeg brannvesenet?
(Vor-dahn kohn-tahk-ter yai brahn-veh-seh-net?)

431. Is there a hospital nearby?
Finnes det et sykehus i nærheten?
(Fee-nes deht eht see-keh-hoos ee nær-heh-ten?)

432. What's the number for poison control?
Hva er nummeret til giftinformasjonen?
(Vah air noo-meh-ret teel geef-tin-for-mah-syoh-nen?)

433. Where can I find a disaster relief center?
Hvor finner jeg et katastrofehjelpsenter?
(Vor feen-ner yai eht kah-tah-stroh-feh-yelp-sen-ter?)

> **Fun Fact:** May 17th is Norway's Constitution Day and is celebrated with parades and festivities.

434. What's the local emergency radio station?
Hva er den lokale nødradio-stasjonen?
(Vah air dehn loh-kah-leh nød-rah-dee-oh-stah-shoh-nen?)

435. Are there any shelters in the area?
Finnes det noen skjul i området?
(Fee-nes deht noh-ehn shool ee ohm-roh-deht?)

436. Who do I call for road assistance?
Hvem ringer jeg for veihjelp?
(Vehm reeng-er yai for vai-hyelp?)

437. How can I reach search and rescue teams?
Hvordan kontakter jeg søk- og redningsteam?
(Vor-dahn kohn-tahk-ter yai søk ohg rehn-neengs-team?)

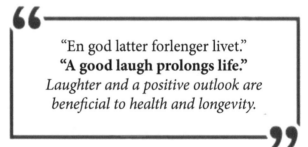

"En god latter forlenger livet."
"A good laugh prolongs life."
*Laughter and a positive outlook are
beneficial to health and longevity.*

Interactive Challenge: Emergencies Quiz

1. **How do you say "emergency" in Norwegian?**

   a) Eple
   b) Nødsituasjon
   c) Ost
   d) Strand

2. **What's the Norwegian word for "ambulance"?**

   a) Bil
   b) Sykkel
   c) Ambulanse
   d) Skole

3. **If you need immediate medical attention, what should you say in Norwegian?**

   a) Jeg vil gjerne ha brød.
   b) Hvor er stasjonen?
   c) Jeg trenger øyeblikkelig medisinsk hjelp.

4. **How do you ask "Is there a hospital nearby?" in Norwegian?**

   a) Hvor er kinoen?
   b) Har du en penn?
   c) Er det et sykehus i nærheten?

5. **What's the Norwegian word for "police"?**

   a) Eple
   b) Politi
   c) Tog

6. **How do you say "fire" in Norwegian?**

    a) Sol
    b) Hund
    c) Brann
    d) Bok

7. **If you've witnessed an accident, what phrase can you use in Norwegian?**

    a) Jeg vil gjerne ha sjokolade.
    b) Jeg har sett en ulykke.
    c) Jeg liker blomster.
    d) Dette er mitt hus.

8. **What's the Norwegian word for "help"?**

    a) Farvel
    b) God dag
    c) Takk
    d) Hjelp!

9. **How would you say "I've been robbed; I need the authorities" in Norwegian?**

    a) Jeg har spist ost.
    b) Jeg har blitt ranet; jeg trenger myndighetene.
    c) Dette er et vakkert fjell.

10. **How do you ask "Can you call an ambulance, please?" in Norwegian?**

    a) Kan du ringe etter en taxi, vær så snill?
    b) Kan du gi meg saltet?
    c) Kan du ringe etter en ambulanse, vær så snill?

11. What's the Norwegian word for "emergency services"?

a) Nødtjenester
b) Deilig kake
c) Lett

12. How do you say "reporting an accident" in Norwegian?

a) Synge en sang
b) Lese en bok
c) Rapportere en ulykke

13. If you need to contact the fire department, what should you say in Norwegian?

a) Hvordan kommer jeg til biblioteket?
b) Jeg må kontakte brannvesenet.
c) Jeg leter etter vennen min.

14. What's the Norwegian word for "urgent"?

a) Liten
b) Vakker
c) Rask
d) Presserende

15. How do you ask for the nearest police station in Norwegian?

a) Hvor er det nærmeste bakeriet?
b) Hvor er den nærmeste politistasjonen?
c) Har du et kart?
d) Hva er klokken?

Correct Answers:

1. b)
2. c)
3. c)
4. c)
5. b)
6. c)
7. b)
8. d)
9. b)
10. c)
11. a)
12. c)
13. b)
14. d)
15. b)

EVERYDAY CONVERSATIONS

- SMALL TALK AND CASUAL CONVERSATIONS -
- DISCUSSING THE WEATHER, HOBBIES, AND INTERESTS -
- MAKING PLANS WITH FRIENDS OR ACQUAINTANCES -

Small Talk

438. How's it going?
      Hvordan går det?
      (Vor-dahn gohr deh?)

439. Nice weather we're having, isn't it?
      Fint vær vi har, ikke sant?
      (Feent vair vee hahr, eek-keh sahnt?)

440. Have any exciting plans for the weekend?
      Har du noen spennende planer for helgen?
      (Hahr doo noh-ehn spen-nehn-deh plah-ner for hel-gen?)

441. Did you catch that new movie?
      Har du sett den nye filmen?
      (Hahr doo seht dehn nee-eh feel-men?)

442. How's your day been so far?
      Hvordan har dagen din vært så langt?
      (Vor-dahn hahr dah-gen deen vairt soh lahngt?)

443. What do you do for work?
      Hva jobber du med?
      (Vah yoh-ber doo mehd?)

444. Do you come here often?
      Kommer du ofte hit?
      (Kom-mer doo ohf-teh heet?)

445. Have you tried the food at this place before?
      Har du prøvd maten her før?
      (Hahr doo pruhvd mah-ten hehr foor?)

446. Any recommendations for things to do in town?
Har du noen anbefalinger til ting å gjøre i byen?
(*Hahr doo noh-ehn ahn-beh-fah-leen-ger teel teeng o yoor-eh ee bee-yen?*)

447. Do you follow any sports teams?
Følger du med på noen sportslag?
(*Fuhl-ger doo mehd poh noh-ehn spohrts-lahg?*)

448. Have you traveled anywhere interesting lately?
Har du reist til noen interessante steder i det siste?
(*Hahr doo ryst teel noh-ehn in-teh-res-sahn-teh steh-der ee deh seest-eh?*)

449. Do you enjoy cooking?
Liker du å lage mat?
(*Lee-ker doo oh lah-geh maht?*)

> **Travel Story:** In a historic wooden church in Røros, a guide described the architecture with "Treet som forteller historier," meaning "The wood that tells stories."

Casual Conversations

450. What's your favorite type of music?
Hva er din favorittmusikk?
(*Vah air deen fah-vo-ritt-moo-see-kk?*)

> **Fun Fact:** Modern skiing originated in Norway; the word "ski" comes from the Old Norse word "skíð."

451.   How do you like to spend your free time?
        Hvordan liker du å tilbringe fritiden din?
        (*Vor-dahn lee-ker doo oh til-breeng-eh free-tee-den deen?*)

452.   Do you have any pets?
        Har du noen kjæledyr?
        (*Hahr doo noh-ehn shay-leh-deer?*)

453.   Where did you grow up?
        Hvor vokste du opp?
        (*Vohr vohk-steh doo opp?*)

454.   What's your family like?
        Hvordan er familien din?
        (*Vor-dahn air fah-mee-lee-ehn deen?*)

455.   Are you a morning person or a night owl?
        Er du en morgenfugl eller en nattugle?
        (*Air doo ehn mohr-gen-foog-l el-ler ehn naht-toog-leh?*)

456.   Do you prefer coffee or tea?
        Foretrekker du kaffe eller te?
        (*For-eh-treh-ker doo kah-fey el-ler teh?*)

457.   Are you into any TV shows right now?
        Ser du på noen TV-serier akkurat nå?
        (*Sehr doo poh noh-ehn teh-veh-seh-ree-er ah-koo-raht noh?*)

        Idiomatic Expression: "Å ha en finger med i spillet." -
        Meaning: "To be involved in something."
        (Literal translation: "To have a finger in the game.")

108

458. What's the last book you read?
Hva er den siste boken du leste?
(*Vah air dehn seest-eh boh-ken doo leh-steh?*)

459. Do you like to travel?
Liker du å reise?
(*Lee-ker doo oh rye-seh?*)

460. Are you a fan of outdoor activities?
Liker du utendørsaktiviteter?
(*Lee-ker doo oo-ten-dohrs-ak-tee-vee-teh-ter?*)

461. How do you unwind after a long day?
Hvordan slapper du av etter en lang dag?
(*Vor-dahn slah-per doo ahv eh-ter ehn lahng dahg?*)

> **Fun Fact:** Brown cheese (brunost) is a unique
> Norwegian dairy product, loved by Norwegians.

Discussing the Weather

462. Can you believe this heat/cold?
Kan du tro denne varmen/kulden?
(*Kahn doo troh dehn-neh vahr-men/kool-dehn?*)

463. I heard it's going to rain all week.
Jeg hørte det skal regne hele uken.
(*Yai hør-teh deht shahl rehg-neh heh-leh oo-ken?*)

464. What's the temperature like today?
Hva er temperaturen i dag?
(*Vah air teh-em-peh-rah-too-ren ee dahg?*)

465. Do you like sunny or cloudy days better?
Foretrekker du solrike eller overskyede dager?
(For-eh-treh-ker doo sohl-ree-keh el-ler oh-ver-she-yeh-deh dah-ger?)

466. Have you ever seen a snowstorm like this?
Har du noen gang sett en slik snøstorm?
(Hahr doo noh-en gahng seht en sheelk snoh-storm?)

467. Is it always this humid here?
Er det alltid så fuktig her?
(Air deht ahl-teed soh fook-teeg hair?)

468. Did you get caught in that thunderstorm yesterday?
Ble du fanget i tordenværet i går?
(Bleh doo fahn-geh ee tohr-den-vair-eh ee gohr?)

469. What's the weather like in your hometown?
Hvordan er været i hjembyen din?
(Vor-dahn air vair-eh ee hyehm-bee-ehn deen?)

470. I can't stand the wind; how about you?
Jeg tåler ikke vinden; hva med deg?
(Yai toh-ler eek-keh vin-den; vah mehd deh?)

471. Is it true the winters here are mild?
Er det sant at vintrene her er milde?
(Air deht sahnt aht vin-treh-neh hair air meel-deh?)

472. Do you like beach weather?
Liker du strandvær?
(Lee-ker doo strahnd-vair?)

473. How do you cope with the humidity in summer?
Hvordan håndterer du fuktigheten om sommeren?
(*Vor-dahn hawn-teh-rer doo fook-teeg-heh-ten ohm sohm-meh-ren?*)

> **Idiomatic Expression:** "Å male fanden på veggen." - Meaning: "To exaggerate the danger of a situation." (Literal translation: "To paint the devil on the wall.")

Hobbies

474. What are your hobbies or interests?
Hva er hobbyene eller interessene dine?
(*Vah air hob-bee-eh-neh el-ler in-teh-res-seh-neh dee-neh?*)

475. Do you play any musical instruments?
Spiller du noen musikkinstrumenter?
(*Speel-ler doo noh-en moo-seek-kin-stroo-mehn-tehr?*)

476. Have you ever tried painting or drawing?
Har du prøvd å male eller tegne?
(*Hahr doo pruhvd oh mah-leh el-ler teh-gneh?*)

477. Are you a fan of sports?
Er du sportsinteressert?
(*Air doo sports-in-teh-res-sehrt?*)

478. Do you enjoy cooking or baking?
Liker du å lage mat eller bake?
(*Lee-ker doo oh lah-geh maht el-ler bah-keh?*)

479.   Are you into photography?
       Er du interessert i fotografering?
       (*Air doo in-teh-res-sehrt ee foh-toh-grah-feh-ring?*)

480.   Have you ever tried gardening?
       Har du prøvd hagearbeid noen gang?
       (*Hahr doo pruhvd hah-geh-ahr-bide noh-en gahng?*)

481.   Do you like to read in your free time?
       Liker du å lese i fritiden din?
       (*Lee-ker doo oh leh-seh ee free-tee-den deen?*)

482.   Have you explored any new hobbies lately?
       Har du utforsket noen nye hobbyer i det siste?
       (*Hahr doo oot-for-sket noh-en nye hob-bee-er ee deht seest-eh?*)

483.   Are you a collector of anything?
       Samler du på noe spesielt?
       (*Sahm-lehr doo poh noh-eh speh-see-elt?*)

484.   Do you like to watch movies or TV shows?
       Liker du å se filmer eller TV-serier?
       (*Lee-ker doo oh seh feel-mer el-ler teh-veh seh-ree-er?*)

485.   Have you ever taken up a craft project?
       Har du noen gang begynt på et håndverksprosjekt?
       (*Hahr doo noh-en gahng beh-gynt poh et hawn-veh-rks-proh-shekt?*)

> **Idiomatic Expression:** "Å slå to fluer i en smekk." -
> Meaning: "To kill two birds with one stone."
> (Literal translation: "To hit two flies in one swat.")

Interests

486. What topics are you passionate about?
Hvilke emner brenner du for?
(Vil-keh em-ner bren-ner doo for?)

487. Are you involved in any social causes?
Er du engasjert i noen sosiale saker?
(Air doo en-gah-shehrt ee noh-en soh-see-ah-leh sah-ker?)

488. Do you enjoy learning new languages?
Liker du å lære nye språk?
(Lee-ker doo oh lær-eh nye sprawk?)

> **Fun Fact:** "Norwegian Wood," a famous Beatles song, refers to the cheap pine wood used to make furniture, not directly to Norway.

489. Are you into fitness or wellness?
Er du opptatt av fitness eller velvære?
(Air doo op-taht ahv fit-ness el-ler vel-veh-reh?)

490. Are you a technology enthusiast?
Er du teknologiinteressert?
(Air doo teh-knoh-loh-gee-in-teh-res-sehrt?)

491. What's your favorite genre of books or movies?
Hva er din favorittsjanger av bøker eller filmer?
(Vah air deen fah-voh-ritt-shahn-ger ahv buh-ker el-ler feel-mer?)

492. Do you follow current events or politics?
Følger du med på aktuelle hendelser eller politikk?
(Fuhl-ger doo mehd poh ak-too-el-leh hen-del-ser el-ler poh-lee-teek?)

493. Are you into fashion or design?
Er du interessert i mote eller design?
(Air doo in-teh-res-sehrt ee mo-teh el-ler deh-sign?)

494. Are you a history buff?
Er du historieinteressert?
(Air doo his-toh-ree-in-teh-res-sehrt?)

495. Have you ever been involved in volunteer work?
Har du noen gang vært involvert i frivillig arbeid?
(Hahr doo noh-en gahng ver-t in-vol-vert ee free-vil-leeg ah-bye?)

496. Are you passionate about cooking or food culture?
Er du lidenskapelig opptatt av matlaging eller matkultur?
(Air doo lee-den-skah-puh-leeg op-taht ahv maht-lah-ging el-ler maht-kool-toor?)

497. Are you an advocate for any specific hobbies or interests?
Forsvarer du noen spesielle hobbyer eller interesser?
(For-svah-rer doo noh-en speh-see-el-leh hob-bee-er el-ler in-teh-res-ser?)

> **Idiomatic Expression:** "Å blåse i noe." -
> Meaning: "To not care about something."
> (Literal translation: "To blow in something.")

Making Plans

498. Would you like to grab a coffee sometime?
Vil du ta en kaffe en gang?
(Vil doo tah en kah-feh en gahng?)

499. Let's plan a dinner outing this weekend.
La oss planlegge en middag ut denne helgen.
(*Lah oss plan-lehg-geh en mid-dahg oot dehn-eh hel-gen.*)

500. How about going to a movie on Friday night?
Hva med å gå på kino fredag kveld?
(*Vah mehd oh gaw paw kee-noh freh-dag kveld?*)

501. Do you want to join us for a hike next weekend?
Vil du bli med oss på en tur neste helg?
(*Vil doo blee mehd oss paw en toor neh-steh helg?*)

502. We should organize a game night soon.
Vi bør organisere en spillkveld snart.
(*Vee bur or-gah-nee-seh-reh en speel-kveld snahrt.*)

503. Let's catch up over lunch next week.
La oss ta igjen over lunsj neste uke.
(*Lah oss tah ee-ghen oh-ver loonsh neh-steh oo-keh.*)

504. Would you be interested in a shopping trip?
Er du interessert i en shoppingtur?
(*Air doo in-teh-res-sehrt ee en shop-ping-toor?*)

505. I'm thinking of visiting the museum; care to join?
Jeg tenker på å besøke museet; vil du bli med?
(*Yai ten-ker paw oh beh-suh-keh moo-seh-et; vil doo blee mehd?*)

506. How about a picnic in the park?
Hva med en piknik i parken?
(*Vah mehd en pee-kneek ee pahr-ken?*)

> **Fun Fact:** The Lærdal Tunnel is the world's longest road tunnel at 24.5 km.

507. Let's get together for a study session.
La oss møtes for en studieøkt.
(*Lah oss muh-tes for en stoo-dee-ukt.*)

508. We should plan a beach day this summer.
Vi bør planlegge en stranddag denne sommeren.
(*Vee bur plan-lehg-geh en strahnd-dahg dehn-neh sohm-meh-ren.*)

509. Want to come over for a barbecue at my place?
Vil du komme over på grillfest hos meg?
(*Vil doo kohm-meh oh-ver paw greel-fest hohs mehg?*)

"Kjærlighet gjør blind."
"Love is blind."
Being in love can make a person overlook flaws.

Interactive Challenge: Everyday Conversations
(Link each English word with their corresponding meaning in Norwegian)

1) Conversation	Småprat
2) Greeting	Språk
3) Question	Samtale
4) Answer	Uformell samtale
5) Salutation	Dialog
6) Communication	Tale
7) Dialogue	Spørsmål
8) Small Talk	Svar
9) Discussion	Kommunikasjon
10) Speech	Hilsen
11) Language	Meningsutveksling
12) Exchange of Opinions	Diskusjon
13) Expression	Dele ideer
14) Casual Conversation	Uttrykk
15) Sharing Ideas	Hilsen

Correct Answers:

1. Conversation - Samtale
2. Greeting - Hilsen
3. Question - Spørsmål
4. Answer - Svar
5. Salutation - Hilsen
6. Communication - Kommunikasjon
7. Dialogue - Dialog
8. Small Talk - Småprat
9. Discussion - Diskusjon
10. Speech - Tale
11. Language - Språk
12. Exchange of Opinions - Meningsutveksling
13. Expression - Uttrykk
14. Casual Conversation - Uformell samtale
15. Sharing Ideas - Dele ideer

BUSINESS & WORK

- INTRODUCING YOURSELF IN A PROFESSIONAL SETTING -
- DISCUSSING WORK-RELATED TOPICS -
- NEGOTIATING BUSINESS DEALS OR CONTRACTS -

Professional Introductions

510. Hi, I'm [Your Name].
Hei, jeg er [Ditt Navn].
(Hay, yai air [Dit Nahvn].)

511. What do you do for a living?
Hva jobber du med?
(Vah yob-ber doo mehd?)

512. What's your role in the company?
Hva er din rolle i selskapet?
(Vah air deen roh-leh ee sel-skah-peht?)

513. Can you tell me about your background?
Kan du fortelle meg om din bakgrunn?
(Kahn doo for-tel-leh may ohm deen bahk-groon?)

514. This is my colleague, [Colleague's Name].
Dette er kollegaen min, [Kollegaens Navn].
(Deh-teh air ko-leh-gah-en meen, [Ko-leh-gah-ens Nahvn].)

515. May I introduce myself?
Kan jeg presentere meg selv?
(Kahn yai preh-sen-teh-reh may selv?)

516. I work in [Your Department].
Jeg jobber i [Din Avdeling].
(Yai yob-ber ee [Deen Ahv-deh-ling].)

517. How long have you been with the company?
Hvor lenge har du vært i firmaet?
(Vohr len-geh hahr doo vehrt ee feer-mah-et?)

518.   Are you familiar with our team?
Kjenner du til teamet vårt?
(*Kyen-ner doo til tea-met vohrt?*)

519.   Let me introduce you to our manager.
La meg introdusere deg for sjefen vår.
(*Lah may in-tro-doo-seh-reh dey for sheh-fen vohr.*)

> **Travel Story:** On a hiking trail in Jotunheimen, a fellow
> hiker pointed to the summit saying, "Toppen er målet,"
> meaning "The peak is the goal."

Work Conversations

520.   Can we discuss the project?
Kan vi diskutere prosjektet?
(*Kahn vee dis-koo-teh-reh pro-shyek-teht?*)

521.   Let's go over the details.
La oss gå gjennom detaljene.
(*Lah oss goh yen-nom deh-tah-yeh-neh.*)

522.   What's the agenda for the meeting?
Hva er agendaen for møtet?
(*Vah air ah-jen-dah-en for moo-teht?*)

523.   I'd like your input on this.
Jeg vil gjerne ha din mening om dette.
(*Yai vil gehr-neh hah deen meh-ning ohm deh-teh.*)

524. We need to address this issue.
Vi må ta tak i dette problemet.
(Vee moh tah tak ee deh-teh pro-bleh-meht.)

525. How's the project progressing?
Hvordan går det med prosjektet?
(Vor-dahn gor deh mehd pro-shek-teht?)

526. Do you have any updates for me?
Har du noen oppdateringer for meg?
(Hahr doo no-en op-dah-teh-rin-ger for may?)

527. Let's brainstorm some ideas.
La oss brainstorme noen ideer.
(Lah oss brain-stor-meh no-en ee-deh-er.)

528. Can we schedule a team meeting?
Kan vi planlegge et teammøte?
(Kahn vee plahn-leh-geh et tehm-muh-teh?)

529. I'm open to suggestions.
Jeg er åpen for forslag.
(Yai air or-pen for for-shlahg.)

Business Negotiations

530. We need to negotiate the terms.
Vi må forhandle om vilkårene.
(Vee moh for-hahn-leh ohm veel-kor-ne.)

531.   What's your offer?
       Hva er tilbudet ditt?
       (*Vah air til-boo-deht dit?*)

532.   Can we find a middle ground?
       Kan vi finne en mellomløsning?
       (*Kahn vee feen-eh en meh-loom-ler-sning?*)

> **Idiomatic Expression:** "Å være i samme båt." -
> Meaning: "To be in the same situation."
> (Literal translation: "To be in the same boat.")

533.   Let's discuss the contract.
       La oss diskutere kontrakten.
       (*Lah oss dis-koo-teh-reh kon-trahk-ten.*)

534.   Are you flexible on the price?
       Er du fleksibel på prisen?
       (*Air doo flek-see-behl poh pree-sen?*)

535.   I'd like to propose a deal.
       Jeg vil gjerne foreslå en avtale.
       (*Yai veel gehr-neh for-eh-sloh en ahv-tah-leh.*)

536.   We're interested in your terms.
       Vi er interessert i dine betingelser.
       (*Vee air in-teh-reh-ser-t ee dee-neh beh-ting-el-ser.*)

537.   Can we talk about the agreement?
       Kan vi snakke om avtalen?
       (*Kahn vee snahk-keh ohm ahv-tah-len?*)

> **Fun Fact:** The aerosol can was invented by a Norwegian
> engineer, Erik Rotheim.

538. Let's work out the details.
La oss jobbe ut detaljene.
(*Lah oss yob-beh oot deh-tah-lee-neh.*)

539. What are your conditions?
Hva er dine betingelser?
(*Vah air dee-neh beh-ting-el-ser?*)

540. We should reach a compromise.
Vi bør komme til enighet.
(*Vee bur kom-meh til eh-nee-het.*)

> **Fun Fact:** The Norwegian Language Council oversees the evolution and integrity of the Norwegian language.

Workplace Etiquette

541. Remember to be punctual.
Husk å være punktlig.
(*Hoosk oh veh-reh poonk-tlee.*)

542. Always maintain a professional demeanor.
Oppretthold alltid en profesjonell holdning.
(*Op-rehthold ahl-teed en pro-feh-sho-nell hold-ning.*)

543. Respect your colleagues' personal space.
Respekter dine kollegers personlige plass.
(*Reh-spek-ter dee-neh kol-leh-gers per-sohn-lee-geh plahss.*)

> **Fun Fact:** Many farms in Norway keep Norwegian Fjord horses, a very old and distinct breed.

544. Dress appropriately for the office.
Kle deg passende for kontoret.
(Kleh deh pah-sen-deh for kon-toh-ret.)

545. Follow company policies and guidelines.
Følg bedriftens policyer og retningslinjer.
(Fuhl bed-rif-tens poh-lee-sy-er oh reht-nings-leen-yer.)

546. Use respectful language in conversations.
Bruk respektfullt språk i samtaler.
(Brook reh-spek-foolt sprawk ee sam-tah-ler.)

547. Keep your workspace organized.
Hold arbeidsområdet ditt organisert.
(Hold ahr-bides-ohm-roh-deh dit or-gah-nee-sert.)

548. Be mindful of office noise levels.
Vær oppmerksom på støynivået på kontoret.
(Vehr op-merk-som poh stoy-nee-vo-et poh kon-toh-ret.)

549. Offer assistance when needed.
Tilby hjelp når det er nødvendig.
(Til-bee yelp nor deh air nur-ven-deeg.)

550. Practice good hygiene at work.
Praktiser god hygiene på jobben.
(Prahk-tee-ser gohd hee-gee-neh poh yob-ben.)

551. Avoid office gossip and rumors.
Unngå sladder og rykter på kontoret.
(Oon-goh slad-der oh rük-ter poh kon-toh-ret.)

Job Interviews

552. Tell me about yourself.
Fortell meg om deg selv.
(For-tell may om day selv.)

553. What are your strengths and weaknesses?
Hva er dine styrker og svakheter?
(Vah air dee-neh steer-ker oh svah-ke-ter?)

554. Describe your relevant experience.
Beskriv din relevante erfaring.
(Beh-skreev deen reh-leh-vahn-teh ehr-fah-ring.)

555. Why do you want to work here?
Hvorfor vil du jobbe her?
(Vor-for veel doo yob-beh hair?)

556. Where do you see yourself in five years?
Hvor ser du deg selv om fem år?
(Vor sair doo day selv ohm fem ohr?)

557. How do you handle challenges at work?
Hvordan håndterer du utfordringer på jobben?
(Vor-dan hawn-teh-rehr doo oot-for-dreen-ger poh yob-ben?)

558. What interests you about this position?
Hva interesserer deg om denne stillingen?
(Vah in-teh-reh-seh-rehr day ohm dehn-eh stee-lingen?)

559. Can you provide an example of your teamwork?
Kan du gi et eksempel på ditt teamarbeid?
(*Kan doo yee et eks-em-pel poh dit team-ar-bayd?*)

560. What motivates you in your career?
Hva motiverer deg i din karriere?
(*Vah mo-tee-veh-rehr day ee deen kah-ree-eh-reh?*)

561. Do you have any questions for us?
Har du noen spørsmål til oss?
(*Hahr doo no-en spurr-smohl teel oss?*)

562. Thank you for considering me for the role.
Takk for at du vurderer meg for denne rollen.
(*Tahk for aht doo vur-dehr-er may for dehn-eh rohlen.*)

Office Communication

563. Send me an email about it.
Send meg en e-post om det.
(*Send may en eh-pohst ohm deht.*)

564. Let's schedule a conference call.
La oss planlegge en telefonkonferanse.
(*Lah oss plan-leg-geh en teh-leh-fohn-kon-feh-rahn-seh.*)

565. Could you clarify your message?
Kan du klargjøre meldingen din?
(*Kan doo klar-yor-eh mel-deen-gen deen?*)

566. I'll forward the document to you.
Jeg vil videresende dokumentet til deg.
(*Yay veell vee-deh-reh-sehn-deh doh-koo-mehn-teht teel day.*)

567. Please reply to this message.
Vennligst svar på denne meldingen.
(*Venn-leegst svar poh dehn-neh mehl-deeng-en.*)

568. We should have a team meeting.
Vi burde ha et teammøte.
(*Vee boor-deh hah eht teahm-mø-teh.*)

> **Idiomatic Expression:** "Å ta noe med en klype salt." -
> Meaning: "To take something with a grain of salt."
> (Literal translation: "To take something with a pinch of
> salt.")

569. Check your inbox for updates.
Sjekk innboksen din for oppdateringer.
(*Shekk inn-bohks-en deen for opp-dah-teh-reeng-er.*)

570. I'll copy you on the correspondence.
Jeg vil kopiere deg på korrespondansen.
(*Yay veell koh-peer-eh day poh kohr-reh-spon-dahn-sen.*)

571. I'll send you the meeting agenda.
Jeg vil sende deg møteagendaen.
(*Yay veell sen-deh day mø-teh-ah-gen-ah-en.*)

572. Use the internal messaging system.
Bruk det interne meldingssystemet.
(*Brook deht een-tehr-neh mehl-deengs-sys-teh-met.*)

573.   Keep everyone in the loop.
        Hold alle oppdatert.
        (*Hohld ah-leh opp-dah-tehrt.*)

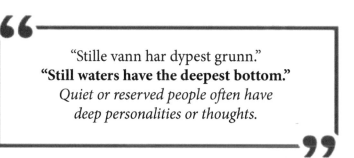

"Stille vann har dypest grunn."
"Still waters have the deepest bottom."
*Quiet or reserved people often have
deep personalities or thoughts.*

Cross Word Puzzle: Business & Work

(Provide the Norwegian translation for the following English words)

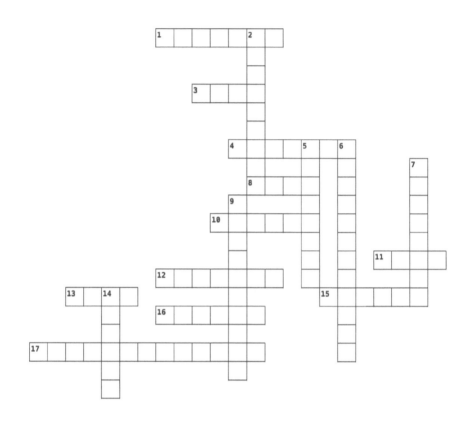

Across

1. - PRODUCT
3. - MEETING
4. - COMPANY
8. - SALARY
10. - OFFICE
11. - BOSS
12. - INCOME
13. - TEAM
15. - EMPLOYEE
16. - CLIENT
17. - MARKETING

Down

2. - CLIENTELE
5. - CONTRACT
6. - PROFESSIONAL
7. - PROJECT
9. - BUSINESS
14. - WORK

Correct Answers:

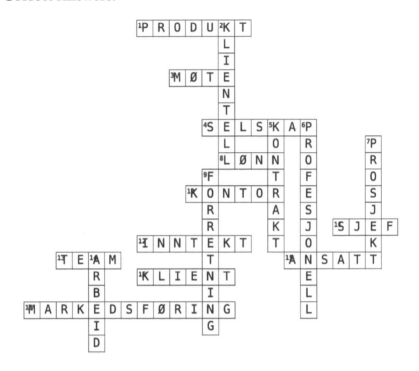

EVENTS & ENTERTAINMENT

- BUYING TICKETS FOR CONCERTS, MOVIES OR EVENTS -
- DISCUSSING ENTERTAINMENT & LEISURE ACTIVITIES -
- EXPRESSING JOY OR DISAPPOINTMENT WITH AN EVENT -

Ticket Purchases

574.   I'd like to buy two tickets for the concert.
Jeg vil kjøpe to billetter til konserten.
(Yay veell shø-peh toh bee-leh-ter teel kon-ser-ten.)

575.   Can I get tickets for the movie tonight?
Kan jeg få billetter til filmen i kveld?
(Kahn yay foh bee-leh-ter teel feel-men ee kvehld?)

576.   We need to book tickets for the upcoming event.
Vi må bestille billetter til det kommende arrangementet.
(Vee moh behs-teel-leh bee-leh-ter teel deh kom-men-deh ah-rahn-jeh-men-teh.)

577.   What's the price of admission?
Hva er inngangsprisen?
(Vah ehr een-gahngs-pree-sehn?)

578.   Do you offer any discounts for students?
Tilbyr dere studentrabatter?
(Teel-beer deh-reh stoo-den-trah-baht-ter?)

579.   Are there any available seats for the matinee?
Er det ledige seter til matineen?
(Ehr deh leh-dee-geh seh-ter teel mah-tee-nehn?)

580.   How can I purchase tickets online?
Hvordan kan jeg kjøpe billetter online?
(Vor-dahn kahn yay shø-peh bee-leh-ter on-line?)

581. Is there a box office nearby?
Er det en billettluke i nærheten?
(*Ehr deh ehn bee-leht-loo-keh ee nær-heh-ten?*)

582. Are tickets refundable if I can't attend?
Kan billetter refunderes hvis jeg ikke kan delta?
(*Kahn bee-leh-ter reh-foon-deh-rehs viss yay eek-keh kahn dehl-tah?*)

583. Can I choose my seats for the show?
Kan jeg velge mine seter til forestillingen?
(*Kahn yay vehl-geh mee-neh seh-ter teel for-eh-stee-leeng-en?*)

584. Can I reserve tickets for the theater?
Kan jeg reservere billetter til teatret?
(*Kahn yay reh-sehr-veh-reh bee-leh-ter teel teh-ah-treh?*)

585. How early should I buy event tickets?
Hvor tidlig bør jeg kjøpe billetter til arrangementet?
(*Vor tee-leeg ber yay shø-peh bee-leh-ter teel ah-rahn-jeh-men-leh?*)

586. Are there any VIP packages available?
Er det noen VIP-pakker tilgjengelige?
(*Ehr deh noo-en V.I.P. pah-ker teel-geng-lee-gehl-eh?*)

587. What's the seating arrangement like?
Hvordan er sitteoppstillingen?
(*Vor-dahn ehr seet-teh-op-stee-leeng-en?*)

> **Idiomatic Expression:** "Å ha grønne fingre." - Meaning: "To have a green thumb."
> (Literal translation: "To have green fingers.")

588.   Is there a family discount for the movie?
        Finnes det familierabatt for filmen?
        (*Feen-nes deh fah-mee-lee-eh-rah-baht for feel-men?*)

589.   I'd like to purchase tickets for my friends.
        Jeg vil kjøpe billetter til vennene mine.
        (*Yay veell shø-peh bee-leh-ter teel veh-nehn-eh mee-neh.*)

> **Fun Fact:** Traditional Norwegian cuisine includes dishes like lutefisk and lefse.

590.   Do they accept credit cards for tickets?
        Aksepterer de kredittkort for billetter?
        (*Auk-sep-teh-rer deh kreh-deet-kort for bee-leh-ter?*)

591.   Are there any age restrictions for entry?
        Er det aldersbegrensninger for inngang?
        (*Ehr deh ahl-ders-beh-gren-seeng-er for een-gahng?*)

592.   Can I exchange my ticket for a different date?
        Kan jeg bytte billetten min til en annen dato?
        (*Kahn yay bee-tteh bee-leh-ten meen teel ehn ahn-nen dah-toh?*)

Leisure Activities

593.   What do you feel like doing this weekend?
        Hva har du lyst til å gjøre denne helgen?
        (*Vah hahr doo leest teel oh yø-reh dehn-neh hehl-gehn?*)

594. Let's discuss our entertainment options.
La oss diskutere underholdningsalternativene våre.
(*Lah ooss dis-koo-teh-reh oon-der-hol-deengs-ahl-tehr-nah-tee-veh-neh voh-reh.*)

> **Fun Fact:** Norway has one of the highest literacy rates in the world.

595. I'm planning a leisurely hike on Saturday.
Jeg planlegger en avslappende tur på lørdag.
(*Yay plahn-leh-ger ehn ahv-slapp-en-deh toor poh løhr-dahg.*)

596. Do you enjoy outdoor activities like hiking?
Liker du utendørsaktiviteter som turgåing?
(*Lee-ker doo oo-ten-dør-sak-tee-vee-teh-ter sohm toor-goh-eeng?*)

597. Have you ever tried indoor rock climbing?
Har du noen gang prøvd innendørs klatring?
(*Hahr doo noo-ehn gahng prøvd een-en-dørs klah-treeng?*)

598. I'd like to explore some new hobbies.
Jeg vil gjerne utforske noen nye hobbyer.
(*Yay veell jehr-neh oot-for-skeh noo-ehn nyeh hob-bee-er.*)

599. What are your favorite pastimes?
Hva er dine favorittpastimer?
(*Vah ehr dee-neh fah-voh-reett-pah-stee-mer?*)

> **Cultural Insight:** Norwegians generally value quietness and personal space, reflecting a respect for individual privacy.

600. Are there any interesting events in town?
Er det noen interessante arrangementer i byen?
(Ehr deh noo-ehn in-teh-reh-sahn-teh ah-ran-jeh-men-ter ee bee-yen?)

601. Let's check out the local art exhibition.
La oss sjekke ut den lokale kunstutstillingen.
(Lah ooss shek-keh oot dehn loh-kah-leh koonst-oot-stee-leen-gen.)

602. How about attending a cooking class?
Hva med å delta på et matlagingskurs?
(Vah mehd oh dehl-tah poh eht maht-lah-geengs-koors?)

603. Let's explore some new recreational activities.
La oss utforske noen nye fritidsaktiviteter.
(Lah ooss oot-for-skeh noo-ehn nyeh free-teeds-ak-tee-vee-teh-ter.)

604. What's your go-to leisure pursuit?
Hva er din foretrukne fritidsaktivitet?
(Vah ehr deen fo-reh-trook-neh free-teeds-ak-tee-vee-teht?)

605. I'm considering trying a new hobby.
Jeg vurderer å prøve en ny hobby.
(Yay voo-reh-dehr oh prø-veh ehn ny hob-bee.)

606. Have you ever attended a painting workshop?
Har du noensinne deltatt på et malekurs?
(Hahr doo noo-ehn-seen-eh dehl-taht poh eht mah-leh-koors?)

Fun Fact: Norway hosted the 41st Chess Olympiad in Tromsø in 2014.

607. What's your favorite way to unwind?
Hva er din favorittmåte å slappe av på?
(*Vah ehr deen fah-voh-ritt-moh-teh oh slap-peh ahv poh?*)

608. I'm interested in joining a local club.
Jeg er interessert i å bli med i en lokal klubb.
(*Yay ehr in-teh-reh-sehrt ee oh bleh mehd ee ehn loh-kahl kloob.*)

609. Let's plan a day filled with leisure.
La oss planlegge en dag fylt med fritid.
(*Lah ooss plahn-lehg-geh ehn dahg feelt mehd free-teed.*)

610. Have you ever been to a live comedy show?
Har du noen gang vært på et live komedieshow?
(*Hahr doo noo-ehn gahng vehrt poh eht lee-veh koh-meh-dee-eh-show?*)

611. I'd like to attend a cooking demonstration.
Jeg vil gjerne delta på en matlagingsdemonstrasjon.
(*Yay veel jehr-neh dehl-tah poh ehn maht-lah-geengs-deh-mohn-strah-syon.*)

> **Fun Fact:** Norway has a vibrant music scene, with genres ranging from black metal to folk and jazz.

Event Reactions

612. That concert was amazing! I loved it!
Den konserten var utrolig! Jeg elsket det!
(*Dehn kohn-sehr-ten vahr oot-roh-leeg! Yay ehl-skeh deh!*)

613. I had such a great time at the movie.
Jeg hadde det kjempegøy på filmen.
(*Yai ha-deh deh shehm-peh-gøy poh feel-men.*)

614. The event exceeded my expectations.
Arrangementet overgikk forventningene mine.
(*Ah-rang-geh-men-teht oh-ver-geek for-vent-neeng-eh-neh mee-neh.*)

615. I was thrilled by the performance.
Jeg var begeistret for forestillingen.
(*Yai vahr beh-guy-streh for for-eh-stee-len-gen.*)

616. It was an unforgettable experience.
Det var en uforglemmelig opplevelse.
(*Deh vahr ehn oo-for-glem-meh-leeg op-leh-vehl-seh.*)

617. I can't stop thinking about that show.
Jeg klarer ikke å slutte å tenke på det showet.
(*Yai klah-rer eek-keh oh sloo-teh oh ten-keh poh deh shoh-et.*)

618. Unfortunately, the event was a letdown.
Dessverre var arrangementet en skuffelse.
(*Dess-vehr-reh vahr ah-rang-geh-men-teht ehn skoof-fehl-seh.*)

619. I was disappointed with the movie.
Jeg var skuffet over filmen.
(*Yai vahr skoof-feht oh-ver feel-men.*)

620. The concert didn't meet my expectations.
Konserten innfridde ikke forventningene mine.
(*Kohn-sehr-tehn in-free-deh eek-keh for-vent-neeng-eh-neh mee-neh.*)

621. I expected more from the exhibition.
      Jeg forventet mer fra utstillingen.
      (*Yai for-ven-teht mehr frah oot-steeling-en.*)

622. The event left me speechless; it was superb!
      Arrangementet gjorde meg målløs; det var fantastisk!
      (*Ah-rang-geh-men-teht yohr-deh mayg mawl-lose; deh vahr fahn-tahs-teesk!*)

623. I was absolutely thrilled with the performance.
      Jeg var helt begeistret for forestillingen.
      (*Yai vahr helt beh-guy-streh for for-eh-steeling-en.*)

> **Idiomatic Expression:** "Å sparke på leggen." -
> Meaning: "To annoy or bother someone."
> (Literally: "To kick on the leg.")

624. The movie was a pleasant surprise.
      Filmen var en hyggelig overraskelse.
      (*Feel-men vahr ehn hee-geh-lee oh-ver-rah-skell-seh.*)

625. I had such a blast at the exhibition.
      Jeg hadde det utrolig gøy på utstillingen.
      (*Yai ha-deh deh oo-troh-leeg gøy poh oot-steeling-en.*)

626. The concert was nothing short of fantastic.
      Konserten var rett og slett fantastisk.
      (*Kohn-sehr-tehn vahr reht oh slett fahn-tahs-teesk.*)

627. I'm still on cloud nine after the event.
      Jeg er fortsatt i syvende himmel etter arrangementet.
      (*Yai ehr fort-saht ee see-ven-deh hee-mel eht ter ah-rang-geh-men-teht.*)

628. I was quite underwhelmed by the show.
Jeg var ganske skuffet over showet.
(*Yai var gahn-skeh skoof-feht oh-ver show-et.*)

629. I expected more from the movie.
Jeg forventet mer fra filmen.
(*Yai for-ven-teht mehr frah feel-men.*)

630. Unfortunately, the exhibition didn't impress me.
Dessverre imponerte utstillingen meg ikke.
(*Dess-veh-rreh im-poh-neh-reh oot-steeling-en mayg eek-keh.*)

> "Å bite over mer enn man kan tygge."
> **"To bite off more than you can chew."**
> *Taking on tasks or responsibilities that are too large to handle.*

Mini Lesson:
Basic Grammar Principles in Norwegian #2

Introduction:

Welcome to the second part of our exploration into Norwegian grammar. Building upon the basics covered previously, this lesson delves deeper into the nuances of Norwegian grammar. These principles are crucial for a thorough understanding of the language, enhancing both your communication skills and comprehension.

1. Sentence Structure:

Norwegian, like English, generally follows a Subject-Verb-Object (SVO) structure. However, the placement of adverbial phrases and other elements can vary:

- *Jeg spiser frokost. (I eat breakfast.)*
- *Spiser du frokost? (Do you eat breakfast?)*
- *I morgen spiser jeg frokost tidlig. (Tomorrow I eat breakfast early.)*

2. Verb Tenses:

Norwegian verbs indicate various tenses including present, past, and future. Perfect and pluperfect tenses are created using the auxiliary verbs "har" (have) and "hadde" (had):

- *Jeg har spist. (I have eaten.)*
- *Jeg hadde spist. (I had eaten.)*

3. Passive Voice:

Passive voice in Norwegian can be formed by adding '-s' to the verb or using the auxiliary verb "bli":

- *Boken leses av studenten. (The book is read by the student.)*
- *Huset ble bygd på 1900-tallet. (The house was built in the 20th century.)*

4. Subordinate Clauses:

In subordinate clauses, the verb often moves to the end:

- *Jeg tror at han bor i Oslo. (I believe that he lives in Oslo.)*
- *Hun sa at hun ville komme. (She said that she would come.)*

5. Infinitive Forms:

To use verbs in the infinitive form, "å" is often placed before the verb, similar to the English "to":

- *Jeg elsker å svømme. (I love to swim.)*
- *Hun trenger å sove. (She needs to sleep.)*

6. Adjectives:

Norwegian adjectives agree with the noun in gender and number, and change form for definite and indefinite usage:

- *En stor bil (a big car) - Indefinite*
- *Den store bilen (the big car) - Definite*

7. Pronouns and Reflexive Verbs:

Norwegian pronouns match in gender and number with their antecedent. Reflexive verbs use "seg" for third-person singular and plural:

- *Han vasker seg. (He washes himself.)*
- *De forbereder seg til festen. (They are preparing themselves for the party.)*

Conclusion:

Grasping these more complex elements of Norwegian grammar will allow you to form sophisticated sentences and deepen your understanding of the language. Regular practice, along with exposure to Norwegian culture and media, will enhance your proficiency. Lykke til! (Good luck!)

HEALTHCARE & MEDICAL NEEDS

- EXPLAINING SYMPTOMS TO A DOCTOR -
- REQUESTING MEDICAL ASSISTANCE -
- DISCUSSING MEDICATIONS AND TREATMENT -

Explaining Symptoms

631.　I have a persistent headache.
Jeg har en vedvarende hodepine.
(Yai har en vehd-vah-ren-deh hoh-deh-pee-neh.)

632.　My throat has been sore for a week.
Jeg har hatt vondt i halsen i en uke.
(Yai har haht vohnt ee hahl-sen ee en oo-keh.)

633.　I've been experiencing stomach pain and nausea.
Jeg har hatt magesmerter og kvalme.
(Yai har haht mah-gehs-mehr-ter ohg kvahl-meh.)

634.　I have a high fever and chills.
Jeg har høy feber og frysninger.
(Yai har hoy feh-ber ohg frees-ning-er.)

635.　My back has been hurting for a few days.
Jeg har hatt vondt i ryggen i noen dager.
(Yai har haht vohnt ee ryg-gen ee noh-en dah-ger.)

636.　I'm coughing up yellow mucus.
Jeg hoster opp gul slim.
(Yai hohs-ter ohpp gool sleem.)

637.　I have a rash on my arm.
Jeg har et utslett på armen.
(Yai har et oot-slet poh ahr-men.)

638.　I feel dizzy and lightheaded.
Jeg føler meg svimmel og ør.
(Yai fur-ler mei sveem-mel ohg ur.)

639. I've been having trouble breathing.
Jeg har hatt problemer med å puste.
(*Yai har haht pro-blem-er mehd oh poos-teh.*)

> **Travel Story:** In a bustling Oslo market, a vendor praised the quality of his wool sweaters with "Norsk kvalitet på sitt beste," meaning "Norwegian quality at its best."

640. My joints are swollen and painful.
Mine ledd er hovne og smertefulle.
(*Mee-neh lehd er hohv-neh ohg smehr-teh-fool-leh.*)

641. I've had diarrhea for two days.
Jeg har hatt diaré i to dager.
(*Yai har haht dee-ah-reh ee toh dah-ger.*)

642. My eyes are red and itchy.
Øynene mine er røde og klør.
(*Oy-neh-neh mee-neh er rur-deh ohg kloor.*)

643. I've been vomiting since last night.
Jeg har kastet opp siden i går kveld.
(*Yai har kahs-tet ohpp see-den ee gohr kveld.*)

644. I have a painful, persistent toothache.
Jeg har en smertefull, vedvarende tannpine.
(*Yai har en smehr-teh-fool, vehd-vah-ren-deh tahn-pee-neh.*)

645. I'm experiencing fatigue and weakness.
Jeg opplever tretthet og svakhet.
(*Yai ohp-lev-er tret-het ohg svahk-het.*)

646. I've noticed blood in my urine.
Jeg har lagt merke til blod i urinen min.
(*Yai har lagt mer-keh til blohd i oo-ree-nen min.*)

647. My nose is congested, and I can't smell anything.
Nesen min er tett, og jeg kan ikke lukte noe.
(*Neh-sen min er tet, oh yai kan eek-keh look-teh noh.*)

648. I have a cut that's not healing properly.
Jeg har et sår som ikke gror riktig.
(*Yai har et sore som eek-keh grohr reek-teeg.*)

649. My ears have been hurting, and I can't hear well.
Ørene mine har vondt, og jeg kan ikke høre godt.
(*Uh-reh-neh mee-neh har vohnt, oh yai kan eek-keh hoo-reh goht.*)

650. I think I might have a urinary tract infection.
Jeg tror jeg kan ha en urinveisinfeksjon.
(*Yai trohr yai kan hah en oo-reen-vais-in-fek-syon.*)

651. I've had trouble sleeping due to anxiety.
Jeg har hatt problemer med å sove på grunn av angst.
(*Yai har haht proh-blem-er mehd oh soh-veh poh groon ahv ahngst.*)

Requesting Medical Assistance

652. I need to see a doctor urgently.
Jeg trenger å se en lege øyeblikkelig.
(*Yai tren-ger oh seh en leh-geh oy-eh-blik-keh-lee.*)

653. Can you call an ambulance, please?
Kan du ringe etter en ambulanse, vær så snill?
(*Kan doo reen-geh et-ter en am-boo-lan-seh, vair soh snill?*)

654. I require immediate medical attention.
Jeg trenger øyeblikkelig medisinsk hjelp.
(*Yai tren-ger oy-eh-blik-keh-lee meh-dee-seensk yelp.*)

655. Is there an available appointment today?
Er det noen ledige timer i dag?
(*Er deh noh-en leh-dee-geh tee-mer ee dahg?*)

656. Please help me find a nearby clinic.
Kan du hjelpe meg med å finne en klinikk i nærheten?
(*Kan doo yel-peh mehg mehd oh feen-eh en klee-neek ee nair-heh-ten?*)

657. I think I'm having a medical emergency.
Jeg tror jeg har en medisinsk nødsituasjon.
(*Yai trohr yai har en meh-dee-seensk nur-see-too-ah-shon.*)

658. Can you recommend a specialist?
Kan du anbefale en spesialist?
(*Kan doo ahn-beh-fah-leh en speh-see-ah-leest?*)

> **Idiomatic Expression:** "Å få vann på mølla." -
> Meaning: "To get more to talk about."
> Literal translation: "To get water on the mill."

659. I'm in severe pain; can I see a doctor now?
Jeg har veldig sterke smerter; kan jeg se en lege nå?
(*Yai har vel-dee ster-keh smehr-ter; kan yai seh en leh-geh noh?*)

660. Is there a 24-hour pharmacy in the area?
Finnes det et døgnåpent apotek i området?
(Feen-nes deh et doughn-oh-pent ah-poh-tek ee ohm-rah-det?)

661. I need a prescription refill.
Jeg trenger en reseptfornyelse.
(Yai trehn-ger en reh-sept-for-nyehl-seh.)

662. Can you guide me to the nearest hospital?
Kan du vise meg veien til nærmeste sykehus?
(Kan doo vee-seh mai vee-ehn til nair-mehs-teh sy-keh-hoos?)

Fun Fact: The Norwegian Forest Cat is a breed of domestic cat originating in Northern Europe.

663. I've cut myself and need medical assistance.
Jeg har skåret meg og trenger medisinsk hjelp.
(Yai har shore meh og trehn-ger meh-dee-seensk yelp.)

664. My child has a high fever; what should I do?
Barnet mitt har høy feber; hva bør jeg gjøre?
(Bahr-net meet har hoy feh-ber; hva bur yai yuh-reh?)

665. Is there a walk-in clinic nearby?
Finnes det en drop-in klinikk i nærheten?
(Feen-nes deh en drop-een klee-neek ee nair-heh-ten?)

666. I need medical advice about my condition.
Jeg trenger medisinske råd om tilstanden min.
(Yai trehn-ger meh-dee-seens-keh rohd om tee-stand-en meen.)

667. My medication has run out; I need a refill.
Medisinene mine er brukt opp; jeg trenger en påfyll.
(*Meh-dee-see-neh-neh mee-neh er brookt opp; yai trehn-ger en poh-feel.*)

668. Can you direct me to an eye doctor?
Kan du henvise meg til en øyelege?
(*Kan doo hen-vee-seh mai til en uh-yeh-leh-geh?*)

669. I've been bitten by a dog; I'm concerned.
Jeg har blitt bitt av en hund; jeg er bekymret.
(*Yai har bleet beet ahv en hoond; yai er beh-keem-ret.*)

670. Is there a dentist available for an emergency?
Finnes det en tannlege tilgjengelig for nødsituasjoner?
(*Feen-nes deh en tan-leh-geh teel-gyen-geh-leeg for nur-see-too-ah-shuh-ner?*)

671. I think I might have food poisoning.
Jeg tror jeg kan ha matforgiftning.
(*Yai trohr yai kan hah maht-for-geeft-neeng.*)

672. Can you help me find a pediatrician for my child?
Kan du hjelpe meg med å finne en barnelege for barnet mitt?
(*Kan doo yel-peh mai mehd oh feen-eh en bar-neh-leh-geh for bahr-net meet?*)

> **Idiomatic Expression:** "Å være en våt klut." -
> Meaning: "To be a wet blanket."
> (Literal translation: "To be a wet cloth.")

Discussing Medications and Treatments

673. What is this medication for?
Hva brukes denne medisinen til?
(Vah broo-kes dehn-neh meh-dee-see-nen teel?)

674. How often should I take this pill?
Hvor ofte skal jeg ta denne pillen?
(Vor of-teh skal yai tah dehn-neh pil-len?)

675. Are there any potential side effects?
Er det noen potensielle bivirkninger?
(Air deh noo-en poh-ten-see-elle bee-veerk-ninger?)

676. Can I take this medicine with food?
Kan jeg ta denne medisinen med mat?
(Kan yai tah dehn-neh meh-dee-see-nen mehd maht?)

677. Should I avoid alcohol while on this medication?
Bør jeg unngå alkohol mens jeg tar denne medisinen?
*(Bur yai oon-noh al-koh-hol mens yai tar dehn-neh
meh-dee-see-nen?)*

678. Is it safe to drive while taking this?
Er det trygt å kjøre bil mens jeg tar dette?
(Air deh trygt oh sure bee-el mens yai tar deh-teh?)

679. How long do I need to continue this treatment?
Hvor lenge må jeg fortsette denne behandlingen?
(Vor len-geh moh yai for-set-teh dehn-neh beh-hand-ling-en?)

680. Can you explain the dosage instructions?
Kan du forklare doseringsinstruksjonene?
(*Kan doo for-klah-reh doh-seh-rings-in-strook-syo-neh-neh?*)

681. What should I do if I miss a dose?
Hva bør jeg gjøre hvis jeg glemmer en dose?
(*Vah bur yai yuh-reh veez yai gleh-mer en doh-seh?*)

682. Are there any dietary restrictions?
Er det noen kostholdsrestriksjoner?
(*Air deh noo-en kohst-holds-res-treek-sho-ner?*)

> **Fun Fact:** The Fjord horse, one of the world's oldest
> breeds, originates from Norway.

683. Can I get a generic version of this medication?
Kan jeg få en generisk versjon av denne medisinen?
(*Kan yai foh en jeh-neh-risk ver-shoon ahv dehn-neh
meh-dee-see-nen?*)

684. Is there a non-prescription alternative?
Finnes det et reseptfritt alternativ?
(*Feen-nes deh et reh-sept-freet al-ter-nah-teev?*)

685. How should I store this medication?
Hvordan bør jeg oppbevare denne medisinen?
(*Vor-dan bur yai ohp-beh-vah-reh dehn-neh meh-dee-see-nen?*)

686. Can you show me how to use this inhaler?
Kan du vise meg hvordan jeg bruker denne inhalatoren?
(*Kan doo vee-seh mai vor-dan yai broo-ker dehn-neh
in-hah-la-toh-ren?*)

687. What's the expiry date of this medicine?
Hva er utløpsdatoen for denne medisinen?
(*Vah air oot-lups-dah-to-en for dehn-neh meh-dee-see-nen?*)

> **Fun Fact:** Norwegian waffles, served heart-shaped, are a popular treat.

688. Do I need to finish the entire course of antibiotics?
Må jeg fullføre hele antibiotikakurset?
(*Moh yai fool-fuh-reh heh-leh an-tee-bee-oh-tee-kah-koo-rseht?*)

689. Can I cut these pills in half?
Kan jeg dele disse pillene i to?
(*Kan yai deh-leh dee-seh pee-leh-neh ee toh?*)

690. Is there an over-the-counter pain reliever you recommend?
Anbefaler du en reseptfri smertestillende?
(*Ahn-beh-fah-lehr doo en reh-sept-free smehr-teh-still-en-deh?*)

691. Can I take this medication while pregnant?
Kan jeg ta denne medisinen mens jeg er gravid?
(*Kan yai tah dehn-neh meh-dee-see-nen mens yai air grah-veed?*)

692. What should I do if I experience an allergic reaction?
Hva bør jeg gjøre hvis jeg får en allergisk reaksjon?
(*Vah bur yai yuh-reh veez yai for en ah-ler-gisk re-ak-syon?*)

> **Fun Fact:** There are a wide variety of dialects spoken in Norway, which can be quite different from each other.

693. Can you provide more information about this treatment plan?
Kan du gi mer informasjon om denne behandlingsplanen?
(*Kan doo gee mair in-for-mah-syon ohm dehn-neh beh-hand-ling-splah-nen?*)

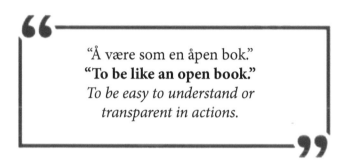

"Å være som en åpen bok."
"To be like an open book."
*To be easy to understand or
transparent in actions.*

Word Search Puzzle: Healthcare

HOSPITAL
SYKEHUS
DOCTOR
LEGE
MEDICINE
MEDISIN
PRESCRIPTION
RESEPT
APPOINTMENT
TIMEAVTALE
SURGERY
KIRURGI
VACCINE
VAKSINE
PHARMACY
APOTEK
ILLNESS
SYKDOM
TREATMENT
BEHANDLING
DIAGNOSIS
DIAGNOSE
RECOVERY
TILFRISKNING
SYMPTOM
SYMPTOM
IMMUNIZATION
IMMUNISERING

```
W  G  M  R  L  R  Q  P  B  F  D  R  R  E  T
H  L  G  E  K  O  N  C  T  W  I  E  G  I  I
N  T  J  P  G  S  W  D  M  T  I  S  N  G  L
K  U  B  P  R  H  C  I  C  N  P  E  I  R  F
P  M  W  U  H  E  Y  B  I  C  L  P  L  U  R
I  C  J  R  H  A  S  I  F  W  J  T  D  R  I
M  O  D  K  Y  S  R  C  K  O  K  V  N  I  S
M  O  T  P  M  Y  S  M  R  U  T  T  A  K  K
Q  R  H  D  N  I  J  E  A  I  K  U  H  C  N
O  U  K  S  W  L  N  C  E  C  P  R  E  X  I
U  G  L  L  X  I  J  H  P  V  Y  T  B  W  N
V  J  G  Y  C  M  E  D  I  S  I  N  I  B  G
R  M  T  I  M  M  U  N  I  Z  A  T  I  O  N
I  I  D  E  L  A  T  V  A  E  M  I  T  V  N
Y  E  A  X  F  R  X  Y  V  A  K  S  I  N  E
M  B  J  S  P  Y  M  S  R  X  B  M  H  I  A
N  S  U  H  E  K  Y  S  B  E  Z  N  L  M  P
G  S  R  Q  A  M  T  H  D  A  G  L  L  Z  O
Z  R  W  E  P  E  O  N  H  J  N  R  A  C  T
E  F  O  T  C  S  S  Z  E  E  B  P  U  S  E
K  M  O  T  P  O  E  Q  S  M  P  E  I  S  K
Q  M  W  I  C  N  V  S  L  O  T  S  E  B  S
L  P  T  F  I  O  Z  E  I  L  O  A  A  X  Q
N  A  U  C  J  Y  D  N  R  N  Z  E  E  N  X
L  S  C  D  J  I  T  L  G  Y  B  G  S  R  C
K  A  H  H  Q  M  U  A  G  R  Q  E  Y  U  T
V  K  S  Y  E  M  I  Z  L  W  C  L  E  T  U
A  O  Z  N  V  D  I  A  G  N  O  S  E  G  R
U  F  T  G  N  I  R  E  S  I  N  U  M  M  I
J  Z  N  M  K  T  G  P  M  L  Q  E  R  Y  V
```

Correct Answers:

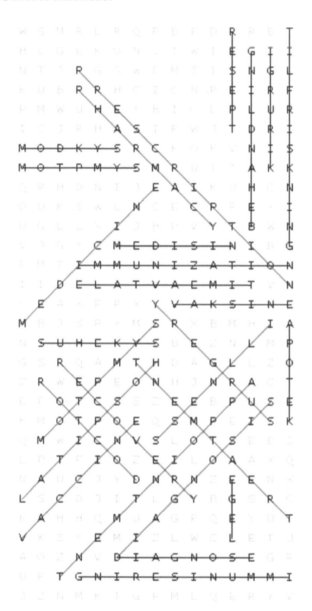

160

FAMILY & RELATIONSHIPS

-TALKING ABOUT FAMILY MEMBERS & RELATIONSHIPS -
- DISCUSSING PERSONAL LIFE & EXPERIENCES -
- EXPRESSING EMOTIONS & SENTIMENTS -

Family Members and Relationships

694. He's my younger brother.
Han er min yngre bror.
(Hahn air meen ung-reh brohr.)

695. She's my cousin from my mother's side.
Hun er min kusine på min mors side.
(Hoon air meen koo-see-neh poh meen mohrs see-deh.)

696. My grandparents have been married for 50 years.
Besteforeldrene mine har vært gift i 50 år.
(Behs-teh-foh-rehl-dreh-neh mee-neh hahr vairt geef-t ee fem-tee ohr.)

697. We're like sisters from another mister.
Vi er som søstre med en annen far.
(Vee air sohm soos-treh mehd ehn ahn-nen fahr.)

698. He's my husband's best friend.
Han er min manns beste venn.
(Hahn air meen mahns behs-teh vehn.)

699. She's my niece on my father's side.
Hun er min niese på min fars side.
(Hoon air meen nee-eh-seh poh meen fahrs see-deh.)

700. They are my in-laws.
De er svigerforeldrene mine.
(Deh air svee-gehr-foh-rehl-dreh-neh mee-neh.)

Fun Fact: The Norwegian Elkhound is one of the ancient Northern Spitz-type breed of dog and is the national dog of Norway.

701. Our family is quite close-knit.
      Familien vår er veldig samholdt.
      (*Fah-mee-lee-ehn vohr air vehl-deeg sahm-hohlt.*)

702. He's my adopted son.
      Han er min adopterte sønn.
      (*Hahn air meen ah-dohp-tehr-teh soonn.*)

703. She's my half-sister.
      Hun er min halvsøster.
      (*Hoon air meen hahlv-soos-tehr.*)

> **Travel Story:** On a foggy morning in the Lofoten Islands, a fisherman described the weather with "Tåke som havets ånde," meaning "Fog like the breath of the sea."

704. My parents are divorced.
      Foreldrene mine er skilt.
      (*Foh-rehl-dreh-neh mee-neh air skeelt.*)

705. He's my fiancé.
      Han er min forlovede.
      (*Hahn air meen fohr-loh-veh-deh.*)

706. She's my daughter-in-law.
      Hun er min svigerdatter.
      (*Hoon air meen svee-gehr-dah-tter.*)

> **Idiomatic Expression:** "Å ha en rød tråd." - Meaning: "To have a consistent theme." (Literal translation: "To have a red thread.")

707.   We're childhood friends.
Vi er barndomsvenner.
(Vee air barn-dohms-vehn-ner.)

708.   My twin brother and I are very close.
Min tvillingbror og jeg er veldig nære.
(Meen tvil-ling-brohr oh yai air vehl-dee nai-reh.)

709.   He's my godfather.
Han er min fadder.
(Hahn air meen fah-der.)

> **Fun Fact:** The Norwegian flag features a blue cross edged in white on a red background.

710.   She's my stepsister.
Hun er min stesøster.
(Hoon air meen steh-søs-ter.)

711.   My aunt is a world traveler.
Tanten min er en verdensreisende.
(Tahn-ten meen air en vehr-dens-rei-sen-deh.)

712.   We're distant relatives.
Vi er fjerne slektninger.
(Vee air fehr-neh slekt-ning-er.)

713.   He's my brother-in-law.
Han er min svoger.
(Hahn air meen svoh-ger.)

714.   She's my ex-girlfriend.
Hun er min ekskjæreste.
(Hoon air meen eks-yai-res-teh.)

Personal Life and Experiences

715. I've traveled to over 20 countries.
Jeg har reist til over 20 land.
(Yai hahr raist til oh-ver tven-tee lahnd.)

716. She's an avid hiker and backpacker.
Hun er en ivrig vandrer og ryggsekkturist.
(Hoon air en ee-vreeg vahn-drer oh rüg-sekk-too-reest.)

717. I enjoy cooking and trying new recipes.
Jeg liker å lage mat og prøve nye oppskrifter.
(Yai lee-ker oh lah-geh maht oh prø-veh nyeh op-skreef-ter.)

718. He's a professional photographer.
Han er en profesjonell fotograf.
(Hahn air en pro-feh-syo-nell fo-to-grahf.)

719. I'm passionate about environmental conservation.
Jeg er lidenskapelig opptatt av miljøvern.
(Yai air lee-den-skah-peh-lee op-taht ahv meel-yø-vern.)

720. She's a proud dog owner.
Hun er en stolt hundeier.
(Hoon air en stolt hoon-dye-er.)

721. I love attending live music concerts.
Jeg elsker å gå på konserter med levende musikk.
(Yai el-skær oh goh poh kon-sair-ter mehd leh-ven-deh moo-seek.)

722. He's an entrepreneur running his own business.
Han er en gründer som driver sin egen forretning.
(Hahn air en grünn-der som dree-ver seen ay-genn for-ret-ning.)

723. I've completed a marathon.
Jeg har fullført en maraton.
(Yai hahr fool-først en mah-rah-ton.)

724. She's a dedicated volunteer at a local shelter.
Hun er en dedikert frivillig på et lokalt herberge.
(Hoon air en deh-dee-kayrt free-vil-leeg poh ett loh-kahlt hair-ber-geh.)

725. I'm a history buff.
Jeg er historieentusiast.
(Yai air hees-toh-ree-ehn-too-see-ahst.)

726. He's a bookworm and a literature lover.
Han er en bokorm og en litteraturelsker.
(Hahn air en boh-korm oh en lit-ter-ah-too-rel-skair.)

727. I've recently taken up painting.
Jeg har nylig begynt å male.
(Yai hahr nil-lee beeg-ünt oh mahl-eh.)

728. She's a film enthusiast.
Hun er en filmelsker.
(Hoon air en feel-mel-skair.)

729. I enjoy gardening in my free time.
Jeg liker å hagearbeide i fritiden min.
(Yai lee-kair oh hah-gair-ar-bye-deh ee free-tee-den meen.)

730.   He's an astronomy enthusiast.
Han er en astronomientusiast.
(*Hahn air en as-troh-noh-mee-ehn-too-see-ahst.*)

731.   I've skydived twice.
Jeg har hoppet i fallskjerm to gangcr.
(*Yai hahr hop-pet ee fahl-shyairm too gahn-ger.*)

732.   She's a fitness trainer.
Hun er en fitnessinstruktør.
(*Hoon air en fit-ness-in-struck-tør.*)

733.   I love collecting vintage records.
Jeg elsker å samle gamle plater.
(*Yai el-skair oh sahm-leh gahm-leh plah-ter.*)

734.   He's an experienced scuba diver.
Han er en erfaren dykker.
(*Hahn air en air-fah-ren düük-kair.*)

735.   I'm a proud parent of three children.
Jeg er en stolt forelder til tre barn.
(*Yai air en stolt for-ell-der til treh barn.*)

> **Fun Fact:** Traditional Norwegian knitwear, like the Mariusgenser, is famous worldwide.

Expressing Emotions and Sentiments

736.   I feel overjoyed on my birthday.
Jeg føler meg veldig glad på bursdagen min.
(*Yai fuh-ler may vehl-dee glahd poh boor-sdah-gen meen.*)

737. She's going through a tough time right now.
Hun går gjennom en tøff periode akkurat nå.
(*Hoon gohr yen-nohm en terf peh-ree-oh-deh ahk-oo-raht noh.*)

738. I'm thrilled about my upcoming vacation.
Jeg er begeistret for min kommende ferie.
(*Yai air by-guys-tret for meen kom-men-deh feh-ree-eh.*)

739. He's heartbroken after the breakup.
Han er knust etter bruddet.
(*Hahn air knoost et-ter broo-det.*)

> **Idiomatic Expression:** "Å ta bladet fra munnen." -
> Meaning: "To speak one's mind."
> (Literal translation: "To take the leaf from the mouth.")

740. I'm absolutely ecstatic about the news.
Jeg er helt ekstatisk over nyheten.
(*Yai air helt ek-stah-teesk oh-ver new-ye-ten.*)

741. She's feeling anxious before the big presentation.
Hun føler seg engstelig før den store presentasjonen.
(*Hoon fur-ler sai eng-steh-lee før dehn stoh-reh preh-sen-tah-sjo-nen.*)

742. I'm proud of my team's achievements.
Jeg er stolt av teamets prestasjoner.
(*Yai air stohlt ahv tea-mehts preh-stah-sho-ner.*)

743. He's devastated by the loss.
Han er ødelagt av tapet.
(*Hahn air ur-deh-lahgt ahv tah-pet.*)

744. I'm grateful for the support I received.
Jeg er takknemlig for støtten jeg mottok.
(*Yai air takk-nehm-lee for stur-ten yai mo-tohk.*)

745. She's experiencing a mix of emotions.
Hun opplever en blanding av følelser.
(*Hoon ohp-leh-ver en blahn-ding ahv fur-leh-ser.*)

746. I'm content with where I am in life.
Jeg er fornøyd med hvor jeg er i livet.
(*Yai air for-nerd mehd hvoohr yai air ee lee-veht.*)

747. He's overwhelmed by the workload.
Han er overveldet av arbeidsmengden.
(*Hahn air oh-ver-vel-det ahv ahr-byds-meng-den.*)

748. I'm in awe of the natural beauty here.
Jeg er i ærefrykt for den naturlige skjønnheten her.
(*Yai air ee eh-reh-frookt for dehn nah-toor-lee-geh shur-nuh-heh-tehn hair.*)

> **Language Learning Tip:** Teach Someone Else - Teaching the basics to someone else can reinforce your own learning.

749. She's relieved the exams are finally over.
Hun er lettet over at eksamenene endelig er over.
(*Hoon air leh-tet oh-ver aht eks-ah-meh-neh-neh en-deh-lee air oh-ver.*)

750. I'm excited about the new job opportunity.
Jeg er spent på den nye jobbmuligheten.
(*Yai air spent poh dehn n-ye yobb-moo-lee-heh-ten.*)

Travel Story: On a scenic train ride to Flåm, a traveler exclaimed, "Eventyrlandskap," meaning "Fairytale landscape."

751. I'm nostalgic about my childhood.
Jeg er nostalgisk over min barndom.
(Yai air no-stahl-gisk oh-ver meen barn-dom.)

752. She's confused about her future.
Hun er forvirret om sin fremtid.
(Hoon air for-veer-ret ohm seen frem-teed.)

753. I'm touched by the kindness of strangers.
Jeg er rørt av fremmedes vennlighet.
(Yai air rurt ahv frem-med-ess ven-lee-het.)

754. He's envious of his friend's success.
Han er misunnelig på vennens suksess.
(Hahn air mee-soon-el-ee poh ven-nens sook-sess.)

755. I'm hopeful for a better tomorrow.
Jeg er håpefull for en bedre morgen.
(Yai air hoh-peh-fool for en beh-dreh mor-gen.)

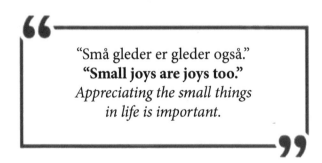

"Små gleder er gleder også."
"Small joys are joys too."
Appreciating the small things in life is important.

Interactive Challenge: Family & Relationships
(Link each English word with their corresponding meaning in Norwegian)

1) Family	Barn
2) Parents	Skilsmisse
3) Siblings	Familie
4) Children	Kjærlighet
5) Grandparents	Vennskap
6) Spouse	Foreldre
7) Marriage	Ektefelle
8) Love	Adopsjon
9) Friendship	Søsken
10) Relatives	Besteforeldre
11) In-laws	Svigerfamilie
12) Divorce	Niese
13) Adoption	Slektninger
14) Cousins	Fettere og kusiner
15) Niece	Ekteskap

Correct Answers:

1. Family - Familie
2. Parents - Foreldre
3. Siblings - Søsken
4. Children - Barn
5. Grandparents - Besteforeldre
6. Spouse - Ektefelle
7. Marriage - Ekteskap
8. Love - Kjærlighet
9. Friendship - Vennskap
10. Relatives - Slektninger
11. In-laws - Svigerfamilie
12. Divorce - Skilsmisse
13. Adoption - Adopsjon
14. Cousins - Fettere og kusiner
15. Niece - Niese

TECHNOLOGY & COMMUNICATION

- USING TECHNOLOGY-RELATED PHRASES -
- INTERNET ACCESS AND COMMUNICATION TOOLS -
- TROUBLESHOOTING TECHNICAL ISSUES -

Using Technology

756. I use my smartphone for various tasks.
Jeg bruker smarttelefonen min for ulike oppgaver.
(Yai broo-ker smart-tele-foh-nen meen for oo-lee-keh op-gah-ver.)

757. The computer is an essential tool in my work.
Datamaskinen er et essensielt verktøy i mitt arbeid.
(Da-ta-mas-kee-nen air et ess-en-si-elt verkt-øy ee meet ar-bayd.)

758. I'm learning how to code and develop software.
Jeg lærer å kode og utvikle programvare.
(Yai lai-rer oh ko-deh og oot-vee-kleh pro-gram-vah-reh.)

759. My tablet helps me stay organized.
Nettbrettet mitt hjelper meg å holde orden.
(Nett-brett-et meet hjel-per may oh hol-deh or-den.)

760. I enjoy exploring new apps and software.
Jeg liker å utforske nye apper og programvare.
(Yai lee-ker oh oot-for-skeh n-yeh ap-per og pro-gram-vah-reh.)

Fun Fact: Bergen is known as the rainiest city in Europe, receiving rain on average 240 days a year.

761. Smartwatches are becoming more popular.
Smartklokker blir stadig mer populære.
(Smart-klok-ker bleer stah-deeg mair pop-oo-lai-reh.)

762. Virtual reality technology is fascinating.
Virtuell virkelighetsteknologi er fascinerende.
(*Veer-choo-ell veer-kel-hee-ehs-tek-no-loh-gee air fas-sin-er-en-deh.*)

763. Artificial intelligence is changing industries.
Kunstig intelligens endrer industrier.
(*Koons-teeg in-tell-ee-gens en-drer in-doos-tree-er.*)

764. I like to customize my gadgets.
Jeg liker å tilpasse mine dingser.
(*Yai lee-ker oh til-pah-seh mee-neh ding-ser.*)

765. E-books have replaced physical books for me.
E-bøker har erstattet fysiske bøker for meg.
(*Eh-bø-ker hahr er-stah-tet fye-si-keh bø-ker for muy.*)

766. Social media platforms connect people worldwide.
Sosiale medieplattformer kobler mennesker over hele verden.
(*So-see-ah-leh meh-dee-eh-platt-for-mer koh-ber men-nes-ker o-ver heh-leh ver-den.*)

767. I'm a fan of wearable technology.
Jeg er fan av bærbar teknologi.
(*Yai air fahn ahv bar-bar tek-no-loh-gee.*)

768. The latest gadgets always catch my eye.
De nyeste dingser fanger alltid oppmerksomheten min.
(*Deh n-yehs-teh ding-ser fahn-ger ahl-teed op-mer-soh-meh-ten meen.*)

769. My digital camera captures high-quality photos.
Mitt digitale kamera tar bilder av høy kvalitet.
(Meet dee-gee-tah-leh kah-meh-rah tahr bil-der ahv hoy kval-ee-tet.)

770. Home automation simplifies daily tasks.
Hjemmeautomatisering forenkler daglige oppgaver.
(Yem-meh-ow-toh-ma-tee-seh-ring foh-renk-ler dahg-lee-geh op-gah-ver.)

771. I'm into 3D printing as a hobby.
Jeg driver med 3D-utskrift som en hobby.
(Yai dree-ver mehd treh-dee-oot-skrift sohm en hob-bee.)

772. Streaming services have revolutionized entertainment.
Strømmetjenester har revolusjonert underholdningen.
(Stro-meh-tyen-ehs-ter hahr reh-vo-loo-syo-nehrt oon-der-hold-nehn.)

773. The Internet of Things (IoT) is expanding.
Internettet av Ting (IoT) utvider seg.
(In-ter-net-tet ahv ting (IoT) oot-vee-der seh.)

774. I'm into gaming, both console and PC.
Jeg er interessert i gaming, både konsoll og PC.
(Yai air in-teh-rehs-ert ee gay-ming, bow-teh kon-soll ohg PC.)

775. Wireless headphones make life more convenient.
Trådløse hodetelefoner gjør livet mer praktisk.
(Trow-luh-seh hoh-deh-teh-leh-foh-ner yur lee-vet mehr prak-tisk.)

> **Fun Fact:** The King Crab is a major seafood export from the northern parts of Norway.

776. Cloud storage is essential for my work.
Skybasert lagring er avgjørende for mitt arbeid.
(Skee-bah-sert lah-gring air ahv-yur-den-deh for meet ar-bayd.)

> **Travel Story:** At a traditional Sami camp in Finnmark, a Sami elder spoke of their ancestral lands with "Hjertet av Sapmi," meaning "The heart of Sapmi."

Internet Access and Communication Tools

777. I rely on high-speed internet for work.
Jeg er avhengig av høyhastighetsinternett for mitt arbeid.
(Yai air ah-ven-gee ahv hoy-has-teegh-ets-in-ter-net for meet ar-bayd.)

778. Video conferencing is crucial for remote meetings.
Videokonferanser er avgjørende for fjernmøter.
(Vee-deh-kon-feh-ran-ser air ahv-yur-den-deh for fyern-mur-ter.)

779. Social media helps me stay connected with friends.
Sosiale medier hjelper meg å holde kontakten med venner.
(So-see-ah-leh meh-dee-er yel-per may oh hol-deh kon-tahk-ten mehd ven-ner.)

780. Email is my primary mode of communication.
E-post er min primære kommunikasjonsmåte.
(Eh-post air meen pree-meh-reh koh-moo-nee-kah-shons-moh-teh.)

781. I use messaging apps to chat with family.
Jeg bruker meldingsapper for å chatte med familien.
(Yai broo-ker mel-deengs-app-er for oh chat-te mehd fah-mee-lee-en.)

782. Voice and video calls keep me in touch with loved ones.
Tale- og videosamtaler holder meg i kontakt med mine kjære.
(Tah-leh oh vee-deh-oh-sahm-tah-ler hohl-der may ee kon-takt mehd meen-eh kyah-reh.)

783. Online forums are a great source of information.
Nettfora er en flott kilde til informasjon.
(Nett-foh-rah air en flott kil-deh teel een-for-mah-syon.)

784. I trust encrypted messaging services for privacy.
Jeg stoler på krypterte meldingstjenester for personvern.
(Yai stoh-ler poh kryp-ter-teh mel-deengs-tyen-est-er for per-sohn-vern.)

785. Webinars are a valuable resource for learning.
Webinarer er en verdifull ressurs for læring.
(Veb-ee-nah-rer air en ver-dee-fool reh-soorss for leh-ring.)

> **Idiomatic Expression:** "Å ta en titt i glasskula." - Meaning: "To predict the future."
> (Literal translation: "To take a look in the crystal ball.")

786. VPNs enhance online security and privacy.
VPN-er forbedrer online sikkerhet og personvern.
(Vee-Pee-En-er for-beh-drer on-line sik-ker-het oh per-sohn-vern.)

787. Cloud-based collaboration tools are essential for teamwork.
Skybaserte samarbeidsverktøy er essensielle for teamarbeid.
(Sky-bas-ter-teh sah-mar-bides-verk-toy air eh-sen-see-elle for tea-mar-bide.)

788. I prefer using a wireless router at home.
Jeg foretrekker å bruke en trådløs ruter hjemme.
(Yai for-eh-trek-ker oh broo-keh en trow-los roo-ter yem-meh.)

789. Online banking simplifies financial transactions.
Nettbank forenkler finansielle transaksjoner.
(Net-bank for-enk-ler fee-nan-see-elle tran-sak-syon-er.)

> **Fun Fact:** Norway offers unique accommodation in ice hotels during winter.

790. VoIP services are cost-effective for international calls.
VoIP-tjenester er kostnadseffektive for internasjonale samtaler.
(Vo-ee-Pe-tyen-est-er air kost-nads-eh-fek-tee-veh for in-ter-nash-yo-nah-leh sam-tah-ler.)

791. I enjoy online shopping for convenience.
Jeg liker netthandel for bekvemmeligheten.
(Yai lee-ker nett-hahn-del for bek-vehm-mel-ee-get-en.)

792. Social networking sites connect people globally.
Sosiale nettverksider knytter mennesker sammen globalt.
(So-see-ah-leh nett-verk-see-der knyt-ter men-nes-ker sahm-men gloh-ballt.)

793. E-commerce platforms offer a wide variety of products.
E-handelsplattformer tilbyr et bredt utvalg av produkter.
(E-han-dels-platt-for-mer til-byrr ett brett oot-vahl av pro-dook-ter.)

> **Idiomatic Expression:** "Å ha rent mel i posen." - Meaning: "To be honest."
> (Literal translation: "To have clean flour in the bag.")

794. Mobile banking apps make managing finances easy.
Mobilbankapper gjør det enkelt å håndtere finanser.
(Mobil-bank-app-er gyor det en-kelt oh hawn-deh-reh fee-nahn-ser.)

795. I'm active on professional networking sites.
Jeg er aktiv på profesjonelle nettverkssider.
(Yai air ak-teev poh pro-fe-syo-nell-e nett-vehrks-see-der.)

796. Virtual private networks protect my online identity.
Virtuelle private nettverk beskytter min online identitet.
(Veer-twel-leh pree-vah-teh nett-vehrk be-skyt-ter meen on-line ee-den-tee-tet.)

797. Instant messaging apps are great for quick chats.
Øyeblikkelige meldingsapper er flotte for raske samtaler.
(Øy-eblikk-eli-ge mel-deengs-app-er air flot-te for rahs-keh sam-tah-ler.)

> **Cultural Insight:** Similar to the Danish 'hygge,' it describes a warm, friendly, and cozy lifestyle, especially during the long winters.

Troubleshooting Technical Issues

798.   My computer is running slow; I need to fix it.
       Datamaskinen min går sakte; jeg må reparere den.
       *(Dah-tah-mah-skee-nen meen gohr sahk-teh; yai moh
       reh-pah-reh-reh den.)*

799.   I'm experiencing network connectivity problems.
       Jeg opplever problemer med nettverkstilkoblingen.
       (Yai op-pleh-ver pro-blem-er mehd nett-vehrks-til-kob-ling-en.)

800.   The printer isn't responding to my print commands.
       Skriveren reagerer ikke på mine utskriftskommandoer.
       *(Skriv-er-en reh-ah-jeer eek-keh poh meen-eh oot-skrifts-kom-
       man-doh-er.)*

       Fun Fact: Norway has a long history of seafaring and
       maritime activities.

801.   My smartphone keeps freezing; it's frustrating.
       Smarttelefonen min fryser stadig; det er frustrerende.
       *(Smart-teh-leh-foh-nen meen fru-ser stah-deeg; det air
       frus-trer-en-deh.)*

802.   The Wi-Fi signal in my house is weak.
       Wi-Fi-signalet i huset mitt er svakt.
       (Vee-Fee sig-na-let ee hoo-set meet air svahkt.)

803.   I can't access certain websites; it's a concern.
       Jeg kan ikke få tilgang til visse nettsider; det er bekymrende.
       *(Yai kahn eek-keh foh til-gang til vis-seh nett-see-der; det air
       be-keem-ren-deh.)*

804. My laptop battery drains quickly; I need a solution.
Batteriet på den bærbare datamaskinen min tømmes raskt; jeg trenger en løsning.
(Bat-ter-ee-et poh den bear-bah-re dah-tah-mah-skee-nen meen tom-mes rahskt; yai treng-er en luh-sning.)

805. There's a software update available for my device.
Det er en programvareoppdatering tilgjengelig for enheten min.
(Det air en pro-gram-vah-re-opp-dah-te-ring til-yen-ge-lee for en-he-ten meen.)

806. My email account got locked; I need to recover it.
E-postkontoen min ble låst; jeg må gjenopprette den.
(Eh-post-kon-to-en meen bleh lost; yai moh yen-op-preh-teh den.)

> **Fun Fact:** Norway is known for its use of wood in traditional architecture.

807. The screen on my tablet is cracked; I'm upset.
Skjermen på nettbrettet mitt er sprukket; jeg er opprørt.
(Shyer-men poh nett-bre-tet meet air spruk-ket; yai air op-rurt.)

808. My webcam isn't working during video calls.
Webkameraet mitt fungerer ikke under videosamtaler.
(Veb-kahm-eh-ret meet foon-ge-rer eek-ke oon-der vee-deo-sam-tah-ler.)

809. My phone's storage is almost full; I need to clear it.
Lagringsplassen på telefonen min er nesten full; jeg må rydde den.
(Lah-grings-plahs-sen poh teh-leh-foh-nen meen air nes-ten fool; yai moh rid-deh den.)

810. I accidentally deleted important files; I need help.
Jeg slettet ved et uhell viktige filer; jeg trenger hjelp.
(*Yai sleh-tet ved ett oo-hell vik-tee-ge fee-ler; yai treng-er yelp.*)

> **Fun Fact:** The Sami people in Norway have their own parliament to manage their affairs.

811. My smart home devices are not responding.
Mine smarte hjemmeenheter reagerer ikke.
(*Meen-eh smar-teh hem-en-he-ter ray-ah-ge-rer eek-ke.*)

812. The GPS on my navigation app is inaccurate.
GPS-en på navigasjonsappen min er unøyaktig.
(*Ge-Pe-Ess-en poh na-vee-gah-shons-ap-pen meen air oo-nyak-tig.*)

813. My antivirus software detected a threat; I'm worried.
Antivirusprogrammet mitt oppdaget en trussel; jeg er bekymret.
(*An-tee-vee-rus-pro-gram-met meet op-dah-get en troo-sel; yai air be-kee-mret.*)

814. The touchscreen on my device is unresponsive.
Berøringsskjermen på enheten min er ikke responsiv.
(*Beh-ru-rings-shyer-men poh en-he-ten meen air eek-ke re-spon-siv.*)

815. My gaming console is displaying error messages.
Spillkonsollen min viser feilmeldinger.
(*Speel-kon-soh-len meen vee-ser fail-mel-din-ger.*)

816. I'm locked out of my social media account.
Jeg er utestengt fra min sosiale medier-konto.
(Yai air oo-teh-stengt frah meen soh-see-ah-leh meh-dee-er kon-toh.)

817. The sound on my computer is distorted.
Lyden på datamaskinen min er forvrengt.
(Loo-den poh dah-tah-mah-skee-nen meen air for-vrengt.)

818. My email attachments won't open; it's frustrating.
Mine e-postvedlegg åpner seg ikke; det er frustrerende.
(Meen-eh e-post-ved-legg oh-pner seh eek-keh; deht air froo-streh-ren-deh.)

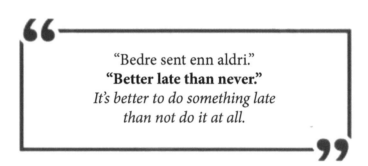

"Bedre sent enn aldri."
"Better late than never."
*It's better to do something late
than not do it at all.*

Cross Word Puzzle: Technology & Communication

(Provide the English translation for the following Norwegian words)

Down

1. - RUTER
2. - KRYPTOLOGI
4. - TASTATUR
6. - SKY
7. - DATA
10. - LADER
11. - INTERNETT
14. - SKJERM

Across

3. - BATTERI
5. - SKRIVER
6. - DATAMASKIN
8. - APPLIKASJONER
9. - WEBKAMERA
12. - LADER
13. - NETTVERK
15. - INNGANG
16. - NETTLESER

Correct Answers:

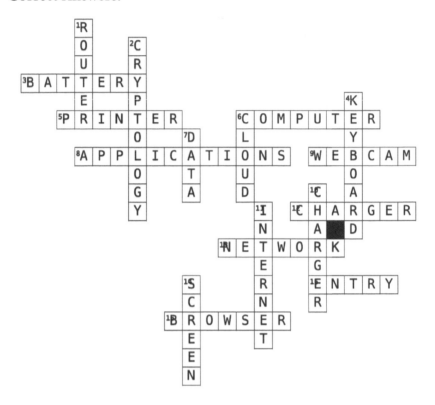

SPORTS & RECREATION

- DISCUSSING SPORTS, GAMES, & OUTDOOR ACTIVITIES -
- PARTICIPATING IN RECREATIONAL ACTIVITIES -
- EXPRESSING ENTHUSUASM OR FRUSTRATION -

Sports, Games, & Outdoor Activities

819. I love playing soccer with my friends.
Jeg elsker å spille fotball med vennene mine.
(Yai el-sker oh spill-eh foot-ball mehd vehn-neh meen-eh.)

820. Basketball is a fast-paced and exciting sport.
Basketball er en rask og spennende sport.
(Bas-ket-ball air en rahsk oh spen-nehn-deh sport.)

821. Let's go for a hike in the mountains this weekend.
La oss gå på en fjelltur denne helgen.
(Lah ohs goh poh en fyell-toor dehn-neh hel-gen.)

822. Playing chess helps improve my strategic thinking.
Å spille sjakk hjelper med å forbedre min strategiske tenkning.
(Oh spill-eh shahk yel-per mehd oh for-beh-dreh meen strah-teh-gis-keh tenk-ning.)

823. I'm a fan of tennis; it requires a lot of skill.
Jeg er en fan av tennis; det krever mye ferdighet.
(Yai air en fahn ahv ten-nis; deht kreh-ver my-eh fehr-di-heit.)

> **Fun Fact:** Norway has more than 1,000 road tunnels, including underwater ones.

824. Are you up for a game of volleyball at the beach?
Er du klar for en volleyballkamp på stranden?
(Air doo klar for en voll-eh-ball-kahmp poh stran-den?)

825.   Baseball games are a great way to spend the afternoon.
Baseballkamper er en flott måte å tilbringe ettermiddagen på.
(Base-ball-kahm-per air en flott moht-teh oh til-bring-eh et-ter-mid-dah-gen poh.)

826.   Camping in the wilderness is so peaceful.
Å campe i villmarken er så fredelig.
(Oh kam-peh ee vill-mar-ken air soh freh-deh-lig.)

827.   I enjoy swimming in the local pool.
Jeg liker å svømme i det lokale bassenget.
(Yai lee-ker oh sveuhm-meh ee deht loh-kah-leh bas-sen-geh.)

828.   Let's organize a game of ultimate frisbee.
La oss organisere en ultimate frisbee-kamp.
(Lah ohs or-gah-nee-sereh en ul-lee-mah-teh fris-bee-kahmp.)

829.   I'm learning to play the guitar in my free time.
Jeg lærer å spille gitar i fritiden min.
(Yai lehr-er oh spill-eh gee-tahr ee free-tee-den meen.)

830.   Skiing in the winter is an exhilarating experience.
Å stå på ski om vinteren er en oppkvikkende opplevelse.
(Oh stoh poh shee ohm vin-teh-ren air en op-kvik-ken-deh op-peh-vehl-seh.)

831.   Going fishing by the lake is so relaxing.
Å fiske ved innsjøen er så avslappende.
(Oh fis-keh vehd in-shuh-ehn air soh ahv-slap-pen-deh.)

832.   We should have a board game night with friends.
Vi burde ha en brettspillkveld med venner.
(Vee boor-deh hah en brett-spill-kveld mehd vehn-ner.)

833. Martial arts training keeps me fit and disciplined.
Trening i kampsport holder meg i form og disiplinert.
(*Tre-ning ee kamp-sport hol-der may ee form oh dis-ee-plee-nairt.*)

834. I'm a member of a local running club.
Jeg er medlem av en lokal løpeklubb.
(*Yai air med-lem ahv en loh-kal luh-peh-klubb.*)

835. Playing golf is a great way to unwind.
Å spille golf er en flott måte å slappe av på.
(*Oh spill-eh golf air en flot moht-eh oh slahp-peh ahv poh.*)

> **Idiomatic Expression:** "Å få på pukkelen." -
> Meaning: "To be reprimanded."
> (Literal translation: "To get on the hump.")

836. Yoga classes help me stay flexible and calm.
Yogatimer hjelper meg å holde meg smidig og rolig.
(*Yo-ga-tee-mer yel-per may oh hol-deh may smee-deeg oh roh-leeg.*)

837. I can't wait to go snowboarding this season.
Jeg kan ikke vente med å dra på snowboard denne sesongen.
(*Yai kahn eek-keh vahn-teh mehd oh drah poh snow-board dehn-neh seh-sohn-gen.*)

838. Going kayaking down the river is an adventure.
Det er et eventyr å padle kajakk nedover elven.
(*Deh air et eh-ven-tewr oh pah-dleh kai-yahkk neh-doh-ver el-ven.*)

839. Let's organize a picnic in the park.
La oss organisere en piknik i parken.
(*Lah ohs or-gah-nee-sereh en peek-neek ee par-ken.*)

Participating in Recreational Activities

840. I enjoy painting landscapes as a hobby.
Jeg liker å male landskap som en hobby.
(Yai lee-ker oh mah-leh lan-skahp sohm en hob-bee.)

841. Gardening is a therapeutic way to spend my weekends.
Hagearbeid er en terapeutisk måte å tilbringe helgene mine på.
(Hah-geh-ahr-bide air en teh-raw-pew-tisk moht-eh oh til-bring-eh hel-ge-neh mee-neh poh.)

842. Playing the piano is my favorite pastime.
Å spille piano er min favoritt fritidsaktivitet.
(Oh spill-eh pee-ah-no air meen fah-vor-eet free-tids-ak-tee-vee-teh.)

843. Reading books helps me escape into different worlds.
Å lese bøker hjelper meg å flykte inn i forskjellige verdener.
(Oh leh-seh buh-ker yel-per may oh flee-kteh inn ee for-she-lig-geh ver-deh-ner.)

844. I'm a regular at the local dance classes.
Jeg er en fast deltaker i de lokale dansekursene.
(Yai air en fast del-tah-ker ee deh loh-kah-leh dan-seh-koo-seh-neh.)

> **Fun Fact:** Oslo was named European Green Capital in 2019 for its dedication to sustainable development.

845. Woodworking is a skill I've been honing.
Trearbeid er en ferdighet jeg har forbedret.
(Treh-ahr-byde air en fehr-dee-ghet yai har for-beh-dret.)

846. I find solace in birdwatching at the nature reserve.
Jeg finner trøst i å se på fugler i naturreservatet.
(*Yai fin-ner trurst ee oh seh poh foogle-er ee nah-toor-re-ser-vah-tet.*)

847. Meditation and mindfulness keep me centered.
Meditasjon og oppmerksomhet holder meg sentrert.
(*Meh-dee-tah-shon ohg opp-merk-som-het hol-der may sen-tert.*)

848. I've taken up photography to capture moments.
Jeg har begynt med fotografering for å fange øyeblikk.
(*Yai har beh-gynt mehd fo-to-grah-feh-ring for oh fahn-geh oy-eh-blikk.*)

849. Going to the gym is part of my daily routine.
Å gå til treningssenteret er en del av min daglige rutine.
(*Oh gaw til treh-ning-sen-teh-ret air en del ahv meen dah-glee-geh roo-tee-neh.*)

850. Cooking new recipes is a creative outlet for me.
Å lage nye oppskrifter er et kreativt utløp for meg.
(*Oh lah-geh nee-yeh opp-skrif-ter air et kre-ah-teevt oot-lurp for may.*)

851. Building model airplanes is a fascinating hobby.
Å bygge modellfly er en fascinerende hobby.
(*Oh byg-geh mo-dell-fly air en fah-si-ner-en-deh hob-bee.*)

852. I love attending art exhibitions and galleries.
Jeg elsker å delta på kunstutstillinger og gallerier.
(*Yai el-sker oh del-tah poh koonst-oote-still-ing-er oh gal-leh-ree-er.*)

853. Collecting rare stamps has been a lifelong passion.
Å samle sjeldne frimerker har vært en livslang lidenskap.
(*Oh sahm-leh shel-dneh free-mer-ker har vairt en leevs-lang lee-den-skahp.*)

854. I'm part of a community theater group.
Jeg er del av en lokalt teatergruppe.
(*Yai air del ahv en loh-kahl teh-ah-ter-groop-peh.*)

855. Birdwatching helps me connect with nature.
Å se på fugler hjelper meg å koble meg til naturen.
(*Oh seh poh foogle-er yel-per may oh koh-bleh may til nah-too-ren.*)

856. I'm an avid cyclist and explore new trails.
Jeg er en ivrig syklist og utforsker nye stier.
(*Yai air en eev-reeg seek-leest oh oot-for-sker nee-yeh stee-er.*)

857. Pottery classes allow me to express myself.
Keramikkurs lar meg uttrykke meg selv.
(*Keh-rah-mikk-oors lahr may oot-tryk-keh may selv.*)

858. Playing board games with family is a tradition.
Å spille brettspill med familien er en tradisjon.
(*Oh spill-eh brett-spill mehd fah-mee-lee-en air en trah-dee-shon.*)

859. I'm practicing mindfulness through meditation.
Jeg praktiserer oppmerksomhet gjennom meditasjon.
(*Yai prak-tee-sehr-er opp-merk-som-het gyen-nom meh-dee-tah-shon.*)

860. I enjoy long walks in the park with my dog.
Jeg liker å ta lange turer i parken med hunden min.
(Yai lee-ker oh tah lahng-eh too-rehr ee pahr-ken mehd hoon-den meen.)

> **Travel Story:** While enjoying a midnight sun hike in Hammerfest, a local described the phenomenon with "Solen som aldri sover," meaning "The sun that never sleeps."

Expressing Enthusiasm or Frustration

861. I'm thrilled we won the championship!
Jeg er begeistret over at vi vant mesterskapet!
(Yai air bai-guy-stret oh-ver ah vee vahnt meh-stehr-shah-peht!)

862. Scoring that goal felt amazing.
Å score det målet føltes utrolig.
(Oh skoh-reh deh moh-let fuhl-tes oot-roh-leeg.)

863. It's so frustrating when we lose a game.
Det er så frustrerende når vi taper en kamp.
(Deh air soh froo-streh-ren-deh nohr vee tah-per en kahmp.)

864. I can't wait to play again next week.
Jeg kan ikke vente med å spille igjen neste uke.
(Yai kahn ee-keh vehn-teh mehd oh speel-leh ee-yen neh-steh oo-keh.)

> **Fun Fact:** In Oslo, the Holmenkollen Ski Jump offers panoramic views of the city.

865. Our team's performance was outstanding.
Lagets prestasjon var enestående.
(*Lah-gets preh-stah-shon vahr eh-neh-stoh-en-deh.*)

866. We need to practice more; we keep losing.
Vi må trene mer; vi taper stadig.
(*Vee moh treh-neh mehr; vee tah-per stah-deeg.*)

867. I'm over the moon about our victory!
Jeg er over månen med vår seier!
(*Yai air oh-ver moh-nen mehd vor se-yehr!*)

> **Language Learning Tip:** Use Sticky Notes - Write words or phrases on sticky notes and place them around your work or study area.

868. I'm an avid cyclist and explore new trails.
Jeg er en ivrig syklist og utforsker nye stier.
(*Yai air en eev-reeg seek-leest ohg oot-for-sker nee-yeh stee-er.*)

869. The referee's decision was unfair.
Dommerens beslutning var urettferdig.
(*Dom-mer-ens beh-sloot-ning vahr oo-reht-fehr-deeg.*)

870. We've been on a winning streak lately.
Vi har vært på en seiersrekke i det siste.
(*Vee hahr vairt poh en se-yehrs-reh-keh ee deh seest-eh.*)

871. I'm disappointed in our team's performance.
Jeg er skuffet over lagets prestasjon.
(*Yai air skoo-fet oh-ver lah-gets preh-stah-shon.*)

872.   The adrenaline rush during the race was incredible.
        Adrenalinkicket under løpet var utrolig.
        (*Ah-dreh-nah-leen-kee-ket oon-der luh-pet vahr oo-troh-leeg.*)

873.   We need to step up our game to compete.
        Vi må heve spillet vårt for å konkurrere.
        (*Vee moh heh-veh speel-let voort for oh kon-koor-reh-reh.*)

                Idiomatic Expression: "Å gå på trynet." -
                Meaning: "To fail spectacularly."
                (Literal translation: "To go on the face.")

874.   Winning the tournament was a dream come true.
        Å vinne turneringen var en drøm som gikk i oppfyllelse.
        (*Oh vin-neh too-ner-ing-en vahr en druhm som geek ee
        ohp-fool-lel-seh.*)

875.   I was so close to scoring a goal.
        Jeg var så nær å score et mål.
        (*Yai vahr soh nair oh skoh-reh ett mohl.*)

876.   We should celebrate our recent win.
        Vi bør feire vår nylige seier.
        (*Vee burh fai-reh voar nee-lee-geh se-yehr.*)

877.   Losing by a narrow margin is frustrating.
        Å tape med liten margin er frustrerende.
        (*Oh tah-peh mehd lee-ten mar-gin air froo-streh-ren-deh.*)

878.   Let's train harder to improve our skills.
        La oss trene hardere for å forbedre ferdighetene våre.
        (*Lah ohs treh-neh har-deh-reh for oh for-beh-dreh fahr-dee-heh-
        teh-neh voar-eh.*)

879. The match was intense from start to finish.
Kampen var intens fra start til slutt.
(*Kam-pen vahr in-tens frah stahrt teel sloot.*)

880. I'm proud of our team's sportsmanship.
Jeg er stolt av sportsånden i laget vårt.
(*Yai air stohlt ahv sports-ohn-den ee lah-get voart.*)

881. We've faced tough competition this season.
Vi har møtt tøff konkurranse denne sesongen.
(*Vee hahr murt toff kon-koo-ran-seh dehn-neh seh-sohn-gen.*)

882. I'm determined to give it my all in the next game.
Jeg er fast bestemt på å gi alt i neste spill.
(*Yai air fuhst beh-stemt poh oh gee ahlt ee neh-steh speel.*)

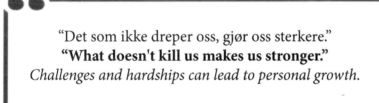

"Det som ikke dreper oss, gjør oss sterkere."
"What doesn't kill us makes us stronger."
Challenges and hardships can lead to personal growth.

Mini Lesson:
Basic Grammar Principles in Norwegian #3

Introduction:

Welcome to the third part of our series on Norwegian grammar principles. Having covered the basics in the previous lessons, we now turn our attention to more advanced aspects of Norwegian grammar. These concepts are vital for a deeper understanding and more effective use of the Norwegian language, enhancing your ability to communicate with greater complexity.

1. Particles:

Norwegian uses particles with verbs to form phrasal verbs. These combinations often have meanings that are not directly related to the individual words.

- *Gå ut (go out)*
- *Slå på (turn on)*
- *Ta av (take off)*

2. Word Formation:

Norwegian allows for the creation of new words through compounding, similar to Danish and other Germanic languages.

- *Tann + børste = Tannbørste (toothbrush)*
- *Skrive + bord = Skrivebord (desk)*

3. Conditional Sentences:

Conditional sentences in Norwegian often use "hvis" (if) and the conditional mood of the verb.

- *Hvis jeg hadde penger, ville jeg reise. (If I had money, I would travel.)*
- *Hvis det regner, blir vi hjemme. (If it rains, we will stay home.)*

4. Reported Speech:

When reporting speech, Norwegian also typically uses a tense backshift.

- *Han sier at han er trøtt. (He says he is tired.)*
- *Hun sa at hun hadde spist. (She said that she had eaten.)*

5. Reflexive Possessive Pronouns:

Norwegian uses reflexive possessive pronouns to clearly indicate ownership, aligning with the subject of the sentence.

- *Han vasker sin bil. (He washes his [own] car.)*
- *De reparerer sitt tak. (They repair their [own] roof.)*

6. The Passive Form:

The passive voice in Norwegian is often formed using the "-s" suffix or the auxiliary verb "bli."

- *Brevet sendes i dag. (The letter is being sent today.)*
- *Huset ble bygget på 1920-tallet. (The house was built in the 1920s.)*

7. Subjunctive Mood:

While not as commonly used in modern Norwegian, the subjunctive mood appears in certain expressions and literary contexts.

- *Leve kongen! (Long live the king!)*
- *Om jeg var rik... (If I were rich...)*

Conclusion:

Mastering these advanced aspects of Norwegian grammar will enable you to form more complex sentences and deepen your understanding of the language's nuances. Regular practice and exposure to Norwegian culture and media remain key to mastering these concepts. Lykke til! (Good luck!)

TRANSPORT & DIRECTIONS

- ASKING FOR AND GIVING DIRECTIONS -
- USING TRANSPORTATION-RELATED PHRASES -

Asking for and Giving Directions

883. Can you tell me how to get to the nearest subway station?
Kan du fortelle meg hvordan jeg kommer til nærmeste t-banestasjon?
(Kahn doo for-tehl-leh may hvohr-dahn yai kom-mer teel nair-meh-steh teh-bah-neh-stah-shoon?)

884. Excuse me, where's the bus stop for Route 25?
Unnskyld, hvor er busstoppet for rute 25?
(Oon-shild, vohr air booss-stop-peht for roo-teh toh-fem?)

885. Could you give me directions to the city center?
Kan du gi meg veibeskrivelse til sentrum?
(Kahn doo yee may vay-bay-shree-vel-seh teel sen-troom?)

886. I'm looking for a good place to eat around here. Any recommendations?
Jeg leter etter et godt sted å spise rundt her. Har du noen anbefalinger?
(Yai leh-ter eh-ter ett goht stehd oh spee-seh roon-t hair. Hahr doo noo-en ahn-beh-fah-lin-ger?)

887. Which way is the nearest pharmacy?
Hvilken vei er det til nærmeste apotek?
(Vil-ken vay air deh teel nair-meh-steh ah-poh-tek?)

888. How do I get to the airport from here?
Hvordan kommer jeg til flyplassen herfra?
(Hvohr-dahn kom-mer yai teel flee-plahs-sen hair-frah?)

889. Can you point me to the nearest ATM?
Kan du vise meg til nærmeste minibank?
(Kahn doo vee-seh may teel nair-meh-steh mee-nee-bahnk?)

890. I'm lost. Can you help me find my way back to the hotel?
Jeg har gått meg vill. Kan du hjelpe meg med å finne veien tilbake til hotellet?
(Yai hahr goht may veell. Kahn doo yehl-peh may mehd oh feen-neh vay-ehn teel-bah-keh teel hoh-teh-leht?)

891. Where's the closest gas station?
Hvor er den nærmeste bensinstasjonen?
(Vohr air dehn nair-meh-steh behn-seen-stah-shoh-nehn?)

892. Is there a map of the city available?
Finnes det et kart over byen tilgjengelig?
(Feen-nes deht ett kahrt oh-vehr by-en teel-yeng-eh-leeg?)

893. How far is it to the train station from here?
Hvor langt er det til togstasjonen herfra?
(Vohr lahngt air deht teel tohg-stah-shoh-nehn hair-frah?)

894. Which exit should I take to reach the shopping mall?
Hvilken utgang bør jeg ta for å nå kjøpesenteret?
(Vil-ken oot-gahng burh yai tah for oh noh sher-peh-sen-teh-reht?)

895. Where can I find a taxi stand around here?
Hvor kan jeg finne en taxiholdeplass i nærheten?
(Vohr kahn yai feen-neh ehn tak-see-hohl-deh-plahss ee nair-heh-tehn?)

896. Can you direct me to the main tourist attractions?
Kan du vise meg veien til de viktigste turistattraksjonene?
(*Kahn doo vee-seh may vay-en teel deh vik-teeg-steh too-reest-ah-trak-shyo-ne-ne?*)

> **Fun Fact:** In Oslo, you can visit the Viking Ship Museum, home to well-preserved Viking ships.

897. I need to go to the hospital. Can you provide directions?
Jeg trenger å gå til sykehuset. Kan du gi meg veibeskrivelse?
(*Yai treng-er oh goh teel seek-eh-hoo-set. Kahn doo yee may vay-bay-shree-vel-seh?*)

898. Is there a park nearby where I can go for a walk?
Er det en park i nærheten hvor jeg kan gå en tur?
(*Air deht en pahrk ee nair-heh-tehn vohr yai kahn goh en toor?*)

899. Which street should I take to reach the museum?
Hvilken gate bør jeg ta for å nå museet?
(*Vil-ken gah-teh burh yai tah for oh noh moo-seh-et?*)

900. How do I get to the concert venue?
Hvordan kommer jeg til konsertstedet?
(*Hvohr-dahn kom-mer yai teel kon-sert-steh-det?*)

901. Can you guide me to the nearest public restroom?
Kan du vise meg til det nærmeste offentlige toalettet?
(*Kahn doo vee-seh may teel deht nair-meh-steh of-fen-tlee-geh toh-ah-leh-tet?*)

902. Where's the best place to catch a cab in this area?
Hvor er det beste stedet å få tak i en taxi i dette området?
(*Vohr air deht beh-steh steh-det oh fo tak ee en tak-see ee deh-teh ohm-raw-det?*)

Buying Tickets

903. I'd like to buy a one-way ticket to downtown, please.
Jeg vil gjerne kjøpe en enveisbillett til sentrum, vær så snill.
(*Yai veel jehr-neh cher-peh en en-vays-bee-lett teel sen-troom, vare soh snil.*)

904. How much is a round-trip ticket to the airport?
Hvor mye koster en tur-retur billett til flyplassen?
(*Vohr myeh kos-ter en toor-reh-toor bee-lett teel flee-plahs-sen?*)

905. Do you accept credit cards for ticket purchases?
Aksepterer dere kredittkort for billettkjøp?
(*Auk-sep-teh-rehr deh-reh kreh-deet-kort for bee-lett-cherp?*)

906. Can I get a student discount on this train ticket?
Kan jeg få studentrabatt på denne togbilletten?
(*Kahn yai fo stoo-dent-rah-baht poh deh-ne tohg-bee-let-ten?*)

907. Is there a family pass available for the bus?
Finnes det et familiepass tilgjengelig for bussen?
(*Feen-nes deht et fah-mee-lee-pass teel-yeng-eh-leeg for boo-sen?*)

> **Travel Story:** In a Kristiansand art gallery, an artist explained her inspiration with "Skjønnheten i det enkle," meaning "The beauty in simplicity."

908. What's the fare for a child on the subway?
Hva er prisen for et barn på t-banen?
(*Vah air pree-sen for et barn poh teh-bah-nen?*)

909. Are there any senior citizen discounts for tram tickets?
Er det noen seniorrabatter for trikkebilletter?
(*Air deh noo-en sen-ee-or-rah-bah-ter for tree-keh-bee-let-ter?*)

910. Do I need to make a reservation for the express train?
Må jeg reservere for hurtigtoget?
(*Moh yai reh-ser-veh-reh for hoor-teeg-toh-get?*)

911. Can I upgrade to first class on this flight?
Kan jeg oppgradere til førsteklasse på denne flygningen?
(*Kahn yai op-grah-deh-reh teel fur-steh-klass-eh poh dehn-neh flee-gning-en?*)

912. Are there any extra fees for luggage on this bus?
Er det ekstra avgifter for bagasje på denne bussen?
(*Air deh ek-strah ahv-geef-ter for bah-gah-sheh poh dehn-neh boo-sen?*)

913. I'd like to book a sleeper car for the overnight train.
Jeg vil gjerne bestille en sovevogn for nattoget.
(*Yai veel yehr-neh beh-stil-leh en soh-veh-vohgn for naht-toh-get?*)

914. What's the schedule for the next ferry to the island?
Hva er tidstabellen for neste ferge til øya?
(*Vah air teeds-tah-beh-len for nehs-teh fehr-geh teel oi-yah?*)

Cultural Insight: Norway has a rich cultural scene with numerous music and arts festivals throughout the year.

915. Are there any available seats on the evening bus to the beach?
Er det ledige seter på kveldsbussen til stranden?
(*Air deh leh-dee-geh seh-ter poh kvelds-boo-sen teel strahn-den?*)

916. Can I pay for my metro ticket with a mobile app?
Kan jeg betale for min t-banebillett med en mobilapp?
(*Kahn yai beh-tah-leh for meen teh-bah-neh-bee-let mehd en moh-beel-app?*)

917. Is there a discount for purchasing tickets online?
Finnes det rabatt ved kjøp av billetter online?
(*Feen-nes deh rah-baht vehd cherp ahv bee-let-ter on-line?*)

918. How much is the parking fee at the train station?
Hvor mye koster parkeringsavgiften ved togstasjonen?
(*Vohr myeh kos-ter pahr-keh-reengs-ahv-geef-ten vehd tohg-stah-shoh-nen?*)

919. I'd like to reserve two seats for the next shuttle bus.
Jeg vil gjerne reservere to seter for neste shuttlebuss.
(*Yai veel yehr-neh reh-ser-veh-reh toh seh-ter for nehs-teh shoot-leh-boos.*)

920. Do I need to validate my ticket before boarding the tram?
Må jeg validere billetten min før jeg går på trikken?
(*Moh yai vah-lee-deh-reh bee-let-ten meen fur yai gohr poh treek-ken?*)

921. Can I buy a monthly pass for the subway?
Kan jeg kjøpe et månedskort for t-banen?
(*Kahn yai cher-peh et moh-neds-kort for teh-bah-nen?*)

922. Are there any group rates for the boat tour?
Finnes det gruppepriser for båtturen?
(*Feen-nes deh groop-eh-pree-ser for boh-toor-en?*)

> **Travel Story:** At an outdoor café in Alesund, a waiter suggested trying the local seafood with "Smaken av havet," meaning "The taste of the sea."

Arranging Travel

923. I need to book a flight to Paris for next week.
Jeg trenger å bestille en flyvning til Paris for neste uke.
(*Yai tren-ger oh beh-stil-leh en fleev-ning teel Pah-ree for neh-steh oo-keh.*)

924. What's the earliest departure time for the high-speed train?
Hva er den tidligste avgangstiden for høyhastighetstoget?
(*Vah air den teed-leeg-steh ahv-gangs-tee-den for hoy-has-teeg-hets-toh-get?*)

925. Can I change my bus ticket to a later time?
Kan jeg endre bussbilletten min til en senere tid?
(*Kahn yai en-dreh boos-bee-let-ten meen teel en seh-neh-reh teed?*)

926. I'd like to rent a car for a week.
Jeg vil gjerne leie en bil for en uke.
(*Yai veel yehr-neh lee-eh en beel for en oo-keh.*)

927. Is there a direct flight to New York from here?
Er det en direkte flyvning til New York herfra?
(*Air deh en dee-rek-teh fleev-ning teel New York hair-frah?*)

928. I need to cancel my reservation for the cruise.
Jeg må avbestille reservasjonen min for cruisct.
(*Yai moh ahv-beh-stil-leh reh-ser-vah-shoh-nen meen for kroo-seh-t.*)

929. Can you help me find a reliable taxi service for airport transfers?
Kan du hjelpe meg å finne en pålitelig taxiservice for flyplasstransport?
(*Kahn doo yel-peh meh oh feen-neh en poh-lee-teh-leeg tak-see-ser-vee-seh for flee-plahss-trahn-sport?*)

930. I'm interested in a guided tour of the city.
How can I arrange that?
Jeg er interessert i en guidet tur rundt i byen. Hvordan kan jeg ordne det?
(*Yai air in-teh-reh-sert ee en gwee-det toor roon-dee ee by-en. Vohr-dahn kahn yai or-deh deh?*)

931. Do you have any information on overnight buses to the capital?
Har du informasjon om nattbusser til hovedstaden?
(*Har doo in-for-mah-shohn ohm naht-boos-ser teel hoh-ved-stah-den?*)

932. I'd like to purchase a travel insurance policy for my trip.
Jeg vil kjøpe en reiseforsikringspolise for turen min.
(*Yai veel cher-peh en ree-seh-for-see-kreengs-po-lee-seh for too-ren meen.*)

> **Cultural Insight:** In the Arctic Circle, the sun doesn't set for part of the summer and doesn't rise for part of the winter.

933. Can you recommend a good travel agency for vacation packages?
Kan du anbefale et godt reisebyrå for feriepakker?
(Kahn doo ahn-beh-fah-leh ett goht rye-seh-byroh for feh-ree-pah-ker?)

934. I need a seat on the evening ferry to the island.
Jeg trenger et sete på kveldsfergen til øya.
(Yai tren-ger ett seh-teh poh kvehlds-fehr-gen teel oy-ah.)

935. How can I check the departure times for international flights?
Hvordan kan jeg sjekke avgangstidene for internasjonale flyvninger?
(Vohr-dahn kahn yai shek-keh ahv-gahngs-tee-deh-neh for in-ter-nah-shoh-nah-leh fleev-ninger?)

936. Is there a shuttle service from the hotel to the train station?
Finnes det en shuttle-service fra hotellet til togstasjonen?
(Feen-nes deh enn shuht-el ser-vees frah hoh-tell-ett teel tohg-stah-shoh-nen?)

937. I'd like to charter a private boat for a day trip.
Jeg vil gjerne leie en privat båt for en dagstur.
(Yai veel yehr-neh lyeh enn pree-vat boht for enn dahgs-toor.)

938. Can you assist me in booking a vacation rental apartment?
Kan du hjelpe meg med å bestille en ferieleilighet?
(Kahn doo yel-peh meh meh ah beh-stil-leh enn feh-ree-ly-leeg-het?)

939. I need to arrange transportation for a group of 20 people.
Jeg må arrangere transport for en gruppe på 20 personer.
(Yai moh ah-ran-yeh-reh trahn-sport for enn groop-peh poh tven-tee per-soh-ner.)

940. What's the best way to get from the airport to the city center?
Hva er den beste måten å komme seg fra flyplassen til sentrum?
(Vah air dehn beh-steh moh-ten oh kohm-meh seh frah flee-plah-sen teel sen-troom?)

941. Can you help me find a pet-friendly accommodation option?
Kan du hjelpe meg å finne et dyrevennlig overnattingsalternativ?
(Kahn doo yel-peh meh oh feen-neh ett dy-reh-vehn-leeg oh-vehr-nah-tings-ahl-ter-nah-teev?)

942. I'd like to plan a road trip itinerary for a scenic drive.
Jeg vil gjerne planlegge en reiserute for en naturskjønn kjøretur.
(Yai veel yehr-neh plahn-lehg-geh enn rye-seh-roo-teh for enn nah-toor-shurn shur-reh-toor.)

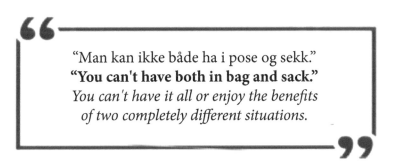

"Man kan ikke både ha i pose og sekk."
"You can't have both in bag and sack."
You can't have it all or enjoy the benefits of two completely different situations.

211

Word Search Puzzle: Transport & Directions

CAR
BIL
BUS
BUSS
AIRPORT
FLYPLASS
SUBWAY
T-BANE
TAXI
TAXI
STREET
GATE
MAP
KART
DIRECTION
RETNING
TRAFFIC
TRAFIKK
PARKING
PARKERING
PEDESTRIAN
FOTGJENGER
HIGHWAY
MOTORVEI
BRIDGE
BRO
ROUNDABOUT
RUNDKJØRING
TICKET
BILLETT

```
O  C  P  O  Q  U  R  Y  J  S  Z  L  A  O  W
Q  P  Y  H  O  V  T  A  X  I  T  K  A  V  C
O  H  N  B  T  R  A  F  I  K  K  R  O  X  B
J  G  S  J  E  F  V  I  E  A  E  V  E  M  Z
S  S  A  L  P  Y  L  F  I  Y  N  N  M  E  K
Y  Q  R  H  Z  Q  E  R  R  U  A  N  D  Z  T
P  L  T  Z  L  N  P  E  P  J  B  T  R  A  K
P  Y  Z  C  J  O  G  X  X  W  P  L  I  E  B
Y  B  I  L  R  D  X  S  A  E  I  M  M  F  D
Q  I  L  T  I  Q  F  Y  D  M  G  I  H  N  E
M  V  C  R  E  G  C  E  A  T  V  J  B  P  C
T  W  B  L  T  D  S  P  T  W  Y  Y  U  C  H
K  X  B  Q  C  T  L  I  O  E  H  Q  S  C  D
T  Q  C  U  R  F  C  R  C  G  U  G  S  T  J
B  R  Q  I  D  K  A  X  I  N  V  P  I  W  M
I  U  A  S  E  C  H  P  I  B  K  W  X  H  P
E  N  S  T  N  S  Y  Q  A  Y  P  A  Q  J  A
V  D  L  B  E  O  J  X  T  R  W  T  E  Z  R
R  K  B  G  F  B  I  K  D  M  K  R  U  U  K
O  J  C  N  O  R  T  T  E  L  L  I  B  D  E
T  Ø  G  I  U  B  O  D  C  M  U  M  N  J  R
O  R  A  N  N  Q  B  U  E  E  G  H  W  G  I
M  I  T  T  G  Z  C  E  N  I  R  X  P  V  N
X  N  E  E  T  I  O  Y  Y  D  D  I  P  Z  G
Y  G  S  R  F  X  B  V  Z  A  A  I  D  B  Z
C  A  Y  F  E  X  E  P  X  A  W  B  B  R  O
V  C  A  I  Z  C  Z  J  Q  L  H  B  O  I  W
M  R  X  Z  V  H  W  Q  D  R  H  W  U  U  B
T  A  R  E  G  N  E  J  G  T  O  F  E  S  T
T  W  V  L  M  P  T  W  D  R  R  I  E  E  V
```

Correct Answers:

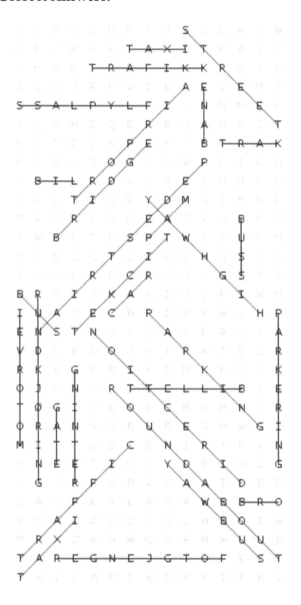

214

SPECIAL OCCASIONS

- EXPRESSING WELL WISHES AND CONGRATULATIONS -
- CELEBRATIONS AND CULTURAL EVENTS -
- GIVING AND RECEIVING GIFTS -

Expressing Well Wishes & Congratulations

943. Congratulations on your graduation!
Gratulerer med fullført utdanning!
(Grah-too-leh-rehr mehd fool-foort oot-dahn-neeng!)

944. Best wishes for a long and happy marriage.
Beste ønsker for et langt og lykkelig ekteskap.
(Behs-teh urns-ker for ett lahngt ohg lyk-ke-lee ek-teh-skap.)

945. Happy anniversary to a wonderful couple.
Gratulerer med dagen til et fantastisk par.
(Grah-too-leh-rehr mehd dah-gen teel ett fahn-tahs-teesk pahr.)

946. Wishing you a speedy recovery.
Ønsker deg en rask bedring.
(Un-sker dey en rahsk beh-drin.)

947. Congratulations on your new job!
Gratulerer med den nye jobben!
(Grah-too-leh-rehr mehd dehn nyeh yoh-ben!)

> **Travel Story:** On a boat tour in Sognefjord, the guide pointed out a waterfall whispering, "Der danser fjellets tårer," meaning "There dance the mountain's tears."

948. May your retirement be filled with joy and relaxation.
Måtte pensjonisttilværelsen din være fylt med glede og avslapning.
(Moh-teh pen-sho-neest-teel-vair-rel-sen deen vah-reh feelt mehd gleh-deh ohg ahv-slahp-neeng.)

949.   Best wishes on your engagement.
Beste ønsker for deres forlovelse.
(*Behs-teh urns-ker for deh-rehs fohr-loh-vel-seh.*)

950.   Happy birthday! Have an amazing day.
Gratulerer med dagen! Ha en fantastisk dag.
(*Grah-too-leh-rehr mehd dah-gen! Hah en fahn-tahs-teesk dahg.*)

> **Cultural Insight:** Saunas are popular in Norway, often located near fjords or lakes for a refreshing swim afterwards.

951.   Wishing you success in your new venture.
Ønsker deg suksess i ditt nye foretak.
(*Un-sker dey soo-ksehs ee deet nyeh foh-reh-tahk.*)

952.   Congratulations on your promotion!
Gratulerer med forfremmelsen!
(*Grah-too-leh-rehr mehd fohr-frehm-mehl-sehn!*)

953.   Good luck on your exam—you've got this!
Lykke til med eksamen – du klarer dette!
(*Luh-keh teel mehd eks-ah-men – doo klah-rer deh-teh!*)

954.   Best wishes for a safe journey.
Beste ønsker for en trygg reise.
(*Behs-teh urns-ker for en treeg ry-seh.*)

955.   Happy retirement! Enjoy your newfound freedom.
God pensjonisttilværelse! Nyt din nyvunne frihet.
(*Gohd pen-sho-neest-teel-vair-rel-seh! Neet deen nee-vun-neh free-het.*)

956. Congratulations on your new home.
Gratulerer med det nye hjemmet.
(Grah-too-leh-rehr mehd deh nye yehm-met.)

957. Wishing you a lifetime of love and happiness.
Ønsker dere et liv fullt av kjærlighet og lykke.
(Un-sker deh-reh ett leev foolt ahv shær-leeg-heet ohg lyk-keh.)

958. Best wishes on your upcoming wedding.
Beste ønsker for deres kommende bryllup.
(Behs-teh urns-ker for deh-res kom-men-deh bryl-loop.)

959. Congratulations on the arrival of your baby.
Gratulerer med ankomsten av deres baby.
(Grah-too-leh-rehr mehd ahn-koms-ten ahv deh-res bah-bee.)

960. Sending you warmest thoughts and prayers.
Sender dere våre varmeste tanker og bønner.
(Sen-der deh-reh voh-reh var-mes-teh tang-ker ohg bun-ner.)

961. Happy holidays and a joyful New Year!
God jul og et gledelig nytt år!
(Gohd yool ohg ett gleh-deh-leeg nytt ohr!)

962. Wishing you a wonderful and prosperous future.
Ønsker dere en fantastisk og velstående fremtid.
(Un-sker deh-reh en fahn-tas-tisk ohg vel-stohn-den-deh frehm-teed.)

Idiomatic Expression: "Å være på tynn is." -
Meaning: "To be in a risky situation."
(Literal translation: "To be on thin ice.")

Celebrations & Cultural Events

963. I'm excited to attend the festival this weekend.
Jeg gleder meg til å delta på festivalen denne helgen.
(Yay gleh-der mey teel oh dehl-tah poh fes-lee-vah-len dehn-neh hel-gen.)

964. Let's celebrate this special occasion together.
La oss feire denne spesielle anledningen sammen.
(Lah oss fye-reh dehn-neh speh-see-el-leh ahn-led-ning-en sahm-men.)

> **Fun Fact:** "Polar Night" is a phenomenon in the north of Norway where the sun doesn't rise above the horizon for months.

965. The cultural parade was a vibrant and colorful experience.
Den kulturelle paraden var en livlig og fargerik opplevelse.
(Dehn kool-toor-el-leh pah-rah-den vahr en lee-vlee ohg fahr-geh-reek oop-lev-els-eh.)

966. I look forward to the annual family reunion.
Jeg ser frem til det årlige familiesamværet.
(Yay ser frehm teel deh ohr-lee-geh fah-mee-lee-sam-veh-ret.)

967. The fireworks display at the carnival was spectacular.
Fyrverkeriet på karnevalet var spektakulært.
(Fyr-ver-kee-ree-et poh kar-neh-vah-let vahr spek-tah-koo-lærht.)

968. It's always a blast at the neighborhood block party.
Det er alltid gøy på nabolagets gatefest.
(Deh ehr ahl-teed goy poh nah-boh-lah-gets gah-teh-fest.)

969. Attending the local cultural fair is a tradition.
Å delta på den lokale kulturmessen er en tradisjon.
(*Oh dehl-tah poh den loh-kah-leh kool-toor-mess-en ehr en trah-dee-shoon.*)

970. I'm thrilled to be part of the community celebration.
Jeg er begeistret for å være en del av samfunnsfeiringen.
(*Yay ehr beh-guys-treh for oh vah-reh en dehl ahv sahm-foons-fay-rin-gen.*)

971. The music and dancing at the wedding were fantastic.
Musikk og dans på bryllupet var fantastisk.
(*Moo-seek ohg dahns poh brul-loop-et vahr fahn-tahs-teesk.*)

972. Let's join the festivities at the holiday parade.
La oss delta i festlighetene under ferieparaden.
(*Lah oss dehl-tah ee fes-tlee-ge-heh-teh oon-der feh-ree-eh-pah-rah-den.*)

973. The cultural exchange event was enlightening.
Kulturutvekslingsarrangementet var opplysende.
(*Kool-toor-oot-veks-lings-ahr-ran-geh-ment-et vahr opp-lee-sen-deh.*)

974. The food at the international festival was delicious.
Maten på den internasjonale festivalen var deilig.
(*Mah-ten poh den in-ter-nah-syo-nah-leh fes-tee-vah-len vahr die-lee.*)

> **Travel Story:** In a Narvik museum, a historian spoke of WWII battles with "Tapperhet under nordlyset," meaning "Bravery under the Northern Lights."

975. I had a great time at the costume party.
Jeg hadde det kjempegøy på kostymefesten.
(Yay hah-deh deh shyem-peh-goy poh kos-tü-meh-fes-ten.)

976. Let's toast to a memorable evening!
La oss skåle for en minneverdig kveld!
(Lah oss skoh-leh for en min-ne-ver-dee kvehld!)

977. The concert was a musical extravaganza.
Konserten var en musikalsk extravaganza.
(Kohn-ser-ten vahr en moo-see-kahlsk eks-tra-va-gahn-zah.)

978. I'm looking forward to the art exhibition.
Jeg ser frem til kunstutstillingen.
(Yay ser frem teel koonst-oot-stil-ling-en.)

979. The theater performance was outstanding.
Teaterforestillingen var enestående.
(Teh-ah-ter-for-eh-stil-ling-en vahr eh-nes-toh-en-deh.)

980. We should participate in the charity fundraiser.
Vi bør delta i innsamlingsaksjonen for veldedighet.
(Vee bør dehl-tah ee in-sahm-ling-ahk-shyon-en for vehl-deh-hee-et.)

981. The sports tournament was thrilling to watch.
Sportsturneringen var spennende å se på.
(Sports-toor-neh-ring-en vahr spehn-en-deh oh se poh.)

982. Let's embrace the local customs and traditions.
La oss omfavne de lokale skikkene og tradisjonene.
(Lah oss ohm-fahv-neh deh loh-kah-leh skee-keh-neh ohg trah-dee-shyo-neh-nuh.)

Giving and Receiving Gifts

983. I hope you like this gift I got for you.
Jeg håper du liker denne gaven jeg fikk til deg.
(Yay haw-per doo lee-ker den-neh gah-ven yay fik til day.)

984. Thank you for the thoughtful present!
Takk for den gjennomtenkte gaven!
(Tahk for den yen-om-tenk-teh gah-ven!)

> **Idiomatic Expression:** "Å ha en finger i paien." -
> Meaning: "To be involved in something."
> (Literal translation: "To have a finger in the pie.")

985. It's a token of my appreciation.
Det er et tegn på min takknemlighet.
(Det air et tei-n poh meen takk-nehm-lee-het.)

986. Here's a little something to brighten your day.
Her er en liten ting for å lyse opp dagen din.
(Hair air en lee-ten ting for oh lee-seh opp dah-gen deen.)

987. I brought you a souvenir from my trip.
Jeg tok med deg en suvenir fra turen min.
(Yay tohk meh day en soo-ve-neer frah too-ren meen.)

988. This gift is for you on your special day.
Denne gaven er til deg på din spesielle dag.
(Den-neh gah-ven air til day poh deen speh-see-elle dahg.)

> **Fun Fact:** Norway is one of the few countries that still
> practices whaling.

989. You shouldn't have, but I love it!
      Du burde ikke ha, men jeg elsker den!
      (Doo boor-deh eek-keh hah, men yay elsker den!)

990. It's a small gesture of my gratitude.
      Det er en liten gest av min takknemlighet.
      (Det air en lee-ten gest ahv meen takk-nehm-lee-het.)

991. I wanted to give you a little surprise.
      Jeg ønsket å gi deg en liten overraskelse.
      (Yay un-sheh-t oh gee day en lee-ten oh-ver-ras-kel-seh.)

992. I hope this gift brings you joy.
      Jeg håper denne gaven gir deg glede.
      (Yay haw-per den-neh gah-ven gear day gleh-deh.)

993. It's a symbol of our friendship.
      Det er et symbol på vennskapet vårt.
      (Det air et see-mbol poh ven-skap-et vort.)

994. This is just a token of my love.
      Dette er bare et tegn på kjærligheten min.
      (Deh-teh air bah-reh et tei-n poh chær-lee-heh-ten meen.)

995. I got this with you in mind.
      Jeg fikk dette med deg i tankene.
      (Yay fik deh-teh meh day ee tah-keh-neh.)

996. I knew you'd appreciate this.
      Jeg visste du ville sette pris på dette.
      (Yay vees-teh doo veel-leh set-teh prees poh deh-teh.)

997. I wanted to spoil you a bit.
      Jeg ville skjemme deg bort litt.
      (Yay veel-leh skyem-meh day bort leet.)

998.   This gift is for your hard work.
       Denne gaven er for ditt harde arbeid.
       (Den-neh gah-ven air for deet hahr-deh ahr-bide.)

999.   I hope you find this useful.
       Jeg håper du finner dette nyttig.
       (Yay haw-per doo fin-ner deh-teh new-tig.)

1000. It's a sign of my affection.
       Det er et tegn på min affeksjon.
       (Det air et tei-n poh meen ah-fek-shoon.)

1001. I brought you a little memento.
       Jeg har med meg en liten suvenir til deg.
       (Yay hahr meh meh en lee-ten soo-veh-neer til day.)

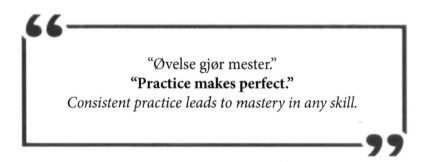

"Øvelse gjør mester."
"Practice makes perfect."
Consistent practice leads to mastery in any skill.

Interactive Challenge: Special Occasions
(Link each English word with their corresponding meaning in Norwegian)

1) Celebration	Festlig
2) Gift	Feiring
3) Party	Bursdag
4) Anniversary	Hilsen
5) Congratulations	Ferie
6) Wedding	Bryllup
7) Birthday	Gave
8) Graduation	Gratulerer
9) Holiday	Uteksaminering
10) Ceremony	Overraskelse
11) Tradition	Skål
12) Festive	Fest
13) Greeting	Seremoni
14) Toast	Tradisjon
15) Surprise	Jubileum

Correct Answers:

1. Celebration - Feiring
2. Gift - Gave
3. Party - Fest
4. Anniversary - Jubileum
5. Congratulations - Gratulerer
6. Wedding - Bryllup
7. Birthday - Bursdag
8. Graduation - Uteksaminering
9. Holiday - Ferie
10. Ceremony - Seremoni
11. Tradition - Tradisjon
12. Festive - Festlig
13. Greeting - Hilsen
14. Toast - Skål
15. Surprise - Overraskelse

CONCLUSION

Congratulations on reaching the final chapter of "The Ultimate Norwegian Phrase Book." As you prepare to traverse the stunning landscapes of Norway, from the majestic fjords to the bustling streets of Oslo, your efforts to master the Norwegian language are truly admirable.

This phrasebook has been your trusty guide, providing key phrases and expressions to facilitate effortless communication. You've journeyed from basic greetings like "Hei" and "God dag" to more intricate phrases, equipping yourself for diverse encounters, enriching experiences, and a deeper connection with Norway's unique culture.

Embarking on the path to language proficiency is an enriching endeavor. Your dedication has laid a robust foundation for fluency in Norwegian. Remember, language is not just a tool for communication but a gateway to understanding a culture's soul and essence.

If this phrasebook has been a part of your language learning adventure, I'd love to hear about it! Connect with me on Instagram: **@adriangruszka**. Share your experiences, seek advice, or just drop a "Hei!" Mentioning this book on social media and tagging me would be greatly appreciated – I am excited to celebrate your progress in mastering Norwegian.

For additional resources, deeper insights, and updates, please visit **www.adriangee.com**. There, you will find a wealth of information, including recommended courses and a supportive community of fellow language enthusiasts eager to aid your ongoing learning journey.

Learning a new language is an exploration into a new world of connections and perspectives. Your enthusiasm for learning and adapting is your greatest tool on this linguistic journey. Seize every opportunity to learn, interact, and deepen your appreciation of the Norwegian way of life.

Lykke til! (Good luck!) Continue practicing with zeal, refining your skills, and most importantly, enjoying every step of your Norwegian language adventure.

Tusen takk! (Thank you very much!) for choosing this phrasebook. May your future explorations be filled with delightful conversations and achievements as you delve further into the fascinating world of languages!

- Adrian Gee

Made in United States
Troutdale, OR
10/15/2024

23779097R00148